An Ahmadiyya Muslim
Autobiography
By: Matiullah Dard

First Edition 2010

Design & Published by:
Nawish Advertising Services Ltd
113 London Road,
Morden,
Surrey SM4 5HP
United Kingdom

ISBN: 978-0-85525-998-3

All rights reserved. No part of this publication may be reproduced, stored in a retrieval system or transmitted in any form or by any means, electronic, mechanical, photo-copying, recording or otherwise, without the prior permission of the Publisher.

£3.00

AN AHMADIYYA MUSLIM

Autobiography
By
Matiullah Dard

TABLE OF CONTENTS

Title	*Page*
1. Dedication	1
2. Preface	2
3. Foreword	3
4. Introduction	4
5. Early Life 1934 - 1960	9
6. Ahmadiyya Mission Fiji	18
7. Preaching Ahmadiyyat in Fiji & New Zealand 1960 - 1963	20
8. Teaching in Birmingham UK 1964 -1999	25
9. The Early History of the Ahmadiyya Muslim Movement in Birmingham UK	27
10. The Dream	32
11. Ahmadiyya Preaching Progress	33
12. Cession of Fiji to Great Britain Centenary Commemoration	43
13. Ahmadiyya Contribution to the Community Health Councils	44
14. The National Schools Committee	48
15. Zia's Persecution of Ahmadies	50
16. Chairman Preaching Committee	55
17. Reverend Billy Graham Challenged	57
18. BBC Radio News	60
19. Reverned Billy Graham Reply to the challenge	64

TABLE OF CONTENTS

Title	*Page*
20. Midlandland Tabligh Seminar & Mubahalah Challenge	66
21. Dar-ul-Barakat	70
22. Nazim Dar-ul-Barakat	71
23. Millennibrum	73
24. Chairman / Postscript	77
25. My Life as a Senior Citizen	79

Miscellanies

26. The Promised Messiah & Imam Mahdi Alaihisslam	81
27. The Royal Observatory Greenwich, London	85
28. Hadhrat Maulana Abdul-Raheem Dard (ra)	88
29. Letters	94
30. Certificates	97
31. News Paper Excerpts	101
32. Friendly Observations	106
33. Glimpses of My Life	108
34. Alfazl Excerpts	120
35. A Letter of Maulana Dost Mohammad Shahid Historian of Ahmadiyyat	123
36. Curriculum Vitae	124
35. Taleem-ul-Islam College Character Certificate	127

*The Promised Messiah &
Imam Mahdi Alaihisslam
1835 - 1908*

Dedication

Grand children:
Aleena, Temoor, Rizwan, Sofia and Zaki.

&

Qosi and Ahmad.

With all my love and prayers. May Allah bless them and keep them loyal and obedient to the Khilafat-e-Ahmadiyya always. Amin.

Matiullah, Qanta Dard, Amtul Rashid & Samiullah
in Qadian 1938

Matiullah Dard at T. I. College
Lahore 1953

Preface

This narrative is a personal account of my life as an Ahmadi Muslim. I accept full responsibility for my interpretation of the events I have recorded and for any omissions or shortcomings.
I have received a great deal of help in compiling this narrative and I would particularly like to thank the following people.
1.   Dr. Ahmad Krishan Dard
2.   Mr. Muzaffar Clarke
3.   Mr. Mohammad Arifin (an Indonesian Ahmadi)

Hadhrat Mirza Nasir Ahmad Khalifatul Masih III (ru)
at London Mosque 1967

**At 63 Melrose Road,
London Mosque**

An Ahmadiyya Muslim 2

BISMILLAH HIRRAHMAN NIRRAHEEM

Foreword

I am extremely delighted to know that my brother Matiullah Dard has compiled the History of Ahmadiyya Jama'at Birmingham. As a matter of fact, this brief autobiography is related to his services rendered to Ahmadiyya Jama'at during his stay at Birmingham.

Mr. Dard is my close friend. Our brotherhood and loving relationship extend over a period of half a century. He has lead, masha Allah, a very active life and has remained always dedicated in the service of Ahmadiyyat. He has inherited this great passion of service for the Jama'at from his elders, including Hazrat Maulana Abdur Reheem Dard.

All members of his family have been sincerely devoted to Ahmadiyya Movement right from its beginning, Alhamado Lillah.

God Almighty would never let go waste sincerity and service; rather He multiplies the reward a thousand fold. As Allah Ta'ala says, "If you are grateful, I will certainly increase my favours upon you." (14:8) Allah has bestowed many favours upon Matiullah Dard, He has granted him good progeny, contentment and peace of mind.

After reading this biography, it becomes obvious, that God Almighty ultimately rewards hard works sincerity and devotion. Allah was his Guide to provide him with opportunities for greater progress in life. His contribution to the welfare of the society has been often reported in the press (a part of which has been included in this book) and has been greatly appreciated by the Local Council of Birmingham.

I pray to Allah for this book to be useful for all readers.

Khaksar
Basheer Ahmad Rafiq
Formerly Imam, Fazl Mosque, London, United Kingdom.

(Rendered into English from Urdu Text by
Dr. Rasheed Sayyed Azam, USA)

Introduction

It is a great honor for me to have been asked by my very learned and eminently qualified teacher, Mr. Matiullah Dard M. A., to write an introduction to his autobiography "An Ahmadiyya Muslim".

In our traditions, words of our teachers (respectfully referred to as masters) are of great importance and immediate compliance is mandatory for the high respect we owe them. As such, I cannot but comply with my master's wish and in doing so I hope to find his approval of my very feeble attempt at writing this brief introduction.

The learned Mr. Dard and I come from two different countries with vastly different backgrounds and yet we have deep underlying connections. He is from Pakistan and I am from the tiny South Pacific island nation of Fiji where Mr. Dard was an English teacher in the early 1960s at the then Lautoka Muslim High School when the secondary schools in the country were still in infancy. The Lautoka Muslim High School, situated in a mosque complex downtown city of Lautoka, essentially catered for the poor students who could not meet the benchmark and make it to the elite Natabua Secondary School (renamed Lautoka High School) and a few of its contemporaries found in the nation during that period.

A graduate of Talimul Islam College (TIC), Rabwah, and University of Punjab, Pakistan, Mr. Dard brought with him a class and style of Oxford. Despite his Punjabi accented English, Mr. Dard had a distinct command and articulation of English language and a superb ability of imparting knowledge. As new high school students, my peers and I were skeptical and very unlearned in the English language. Within two short semesters the gifted Mr. Dard quickly equipped us with the core part of the English grammar that became forever part of our language skill sufficient to help us write and speak clear English. I remember Mr. Dard once read out one my essays on picnic to the whole class. I had rewritten the essay from a student contribution in the Viveka Nanda High School magazine. Mr. Dard's kind gesture motivated me greatly and inspired me to take to writing and public speaking.

The following year 1963, we were looking forward to Mr. Dard's continued rewarding instructions in English for our first effort at the Fiji Junior Examination. Little did we know that Mr. Dard had moved on and left the country on another assignment. We were devastated and heart-broken more so because the teachers who filled in did not have the quality, the charisma and the ability that

Mr. Dard possessed. Mr. Dard left us a lasting impression of himself and often we talked about how great a teacher he was.

In 1965 when I took to teaching at the Lautoka Muslim Elementary School, I met a most loving friend and mentor Master Muhammad Hussain, the deputy principal of the school, who introduced me to the Ahmadiyya Muslim Jamaat. I subsequently accepted the initiation (that was supposed to have been done at the blessed hands of late Sir Muhammad Zafrullah Khan) and congregated at late Lala Mohammed Sidique Khan's residence downtown for the Jumah prayers. It was here I heard of Mr. Dard's name quite frequently mentioned by late Sidique Khan, his wife and sons, Zafrullah Khan, Khairullah Khan, Niyamatullah Khan and Asmatullah Khan whose brotherly affections I enjoyed most overwhelmingly. It was here I also met the first Ahmadiyya Muslim missionary to the Fiji Islands, the late Maulana Sheikh Abdul Wahid Sahib, Mr. Dard refers to him in his autobiography with whom he allied in forming the Jamaat. I was amazed at this revelation that Mr. Dard was also an Ahmadi Muslim and I wanted to reach out to him and convey him the good news that I was with him being the humble follower of Hazrat Masih-e-Moaud.

It has been about forty years I have been trying to reach him A letter I sent him to the London Mosque address never seems to have reached him. Amazingly, the advent of internet has changed the whole dynamics of communication, search and research of things almost in any part of the world just by the click of a button. I was deeply moved and felt immensely grateful to Allah when Mr. Dard sent me an email a few weeks ago while he was visiting his son Dr. Ahmad Kirshan Dard in North Carolina to say how impressed he was with some of my writings I posted on my website and several blogs on Ahmadiyya the true Islam.

In our email exchanges, Mr. Dard directed my attention to his website www.matiullahdard.tripod.com which carries his autobiography and asked for my opinion. I found the work extremely informative and a detail narrative of how he spent the "missed" forty years in England as an educator, promoter of Urdu language and working ceaselessly for the Ahmadiyya Muslim Jamaat in various capacities.

Where the Fiji Muslim League failed to gain from the talent and skills of Mr. Dard to promote Urdu language at college level, Mr. Dard's new place, Birmingham, gave him the liberty and opportunity to give full expression to his expertise in teaching and promoting Urdu language to everyone without regard to color, creed or nationality. The English newspapers gave Mr. Dard raving reviews of selfless endeavors on his retirement.

As an ardent soldier of Islam and proud emissary of most peaceful and resolutely dedicated Jamaat Ahmadiyya, Mr. Dard's passion for Ahmadiyyat the true Islam first took him to Fiji. In the Ahmadiyya sect of Islam, we strongly believe in prayers as the key to all our success. All successful Ahmadi Muslims like Mr. Dard bear testimony to the fact that our prayers have a special acceptance in the courtyard of Allah not because we possess any special qualities but because it is the promise of Allah to His Masih and Mehdi that He will bless them with extraordinary success for believing in the Imam of the age Hazrat Mirza Ghulam Ahmad (peace be upon him) for the rejuvenation of the faith.

I feel extremely honored to learn that my name found mention in a letter Maulana Sheikh Abdul Wahid sahib, the first Ahmadiyya Muslim missionary to Fiji, wrote to Mr. Dard when I joined the Jamaat as a teenager in defiance of the Koya family traditions.

I can imagine the initial challenges Mr. Dard and Maulana Sheikh Abdul Wahid sahib must have faced in their efforts to convincing members of the Lahore Ahmadies who already existed in Fiji since 1930s due in part to the reactions to the Shudhi campaign in Fiji.

In the early 1930s the Fiji Hindu community had been influenced by a visiting Hindu priest to launch a Shudhi campaign, similar to the one that was contemporaneously being carried out in India, to covert Muslims to the Hindu faith. A group of concerned Fiji Muslims, among them my late grandfather Al Haj Moidin Koya, decided to take action to thwart the Shudhi campaign and to curtail further conversion. The group placed Ads in Indian newspapers and actively sought services of a Muslim cleric versed in Islamic studies, Hindu literature and Sanskrit. The only respondent was Maulana Abdul Haq Vidhayarti who happened to be a member of the Ahmadiyya Jamaat Lahore.

The Maulana sahib did succeed in turning the table on the Shudhi campaigners. However, he got exposed as an Ahmadi and before he departed Fiji he had organized the first Lahore Jamaat under the name of Anjuman Ishaat-e-Islam. The group that had invited Abdul Haq Vidhayarti later crystallized in to what is now known as The Fiji Muslim League today.

As usual, the Lahore Ahmadies in Fiji were not fully exposed to the concept of Khilafat and the Amir system that we as mainstream Ahmadiyya Muslim Community are familiar with and deeply loyal to. In some circles though, those who took to serious reading of Hazrat Masih-e-Maoud's writings specially Haqeeqatul Wahi, there were some discussions and curiosity of Hazur's claim to prophet hood and Khilafat. Late Haji Ramzan Khan, a landlord of Nadi Town in Fiji, was one of them whose inquiries led him to Rabwah , Pakistan in 1960 where Haji Ramzan Khan met Hazrat Khalifatul Masih II and pledged at his blessed hands. It was at the direction of Hazrat Khalifatul Masih II, Mr. Dard married a granddaughter of Haji Ramzan Khan and undertook a journey to Fiji to work in close conjunction with Maulana Sheikh Abdul Wahid sahib in Tabligh-e-Ahmadiyyat.

It was the progeny of this group, the second generation of indentured Indian laborers to Fiji, that M. Dard and Maulana Sheikh Abdul Wahib sahib focused on. Although Mr. Dard left Fiji for further studies and to settle in Birmingham, England, his efforts paved a clear path to winning more Lahore Ahmadies to the Fiji Jamaat in later years. When Hazrat Khalifatul Masih IV made his maiden visit to Fiji in 1984, most Lahore Ahmadies with the exception of a few, joined our Jamaat.

Prayers are a mainstay for every successful Ahmadi Muslim in the world. Mr. Dard is no exception and he clearly alludes to this when he is faced with legal situation to visit New Zealand without a visa. Coupled with his prayers and use of diplomatic contacts Mr. Dard had made in Fiji, among them Fijian embassy staff and the then Governor of Fiji Sir Kenneth Medock, all of which seemed to have work as a miracle to induce the New Zealand Immigration to relax conditions and grant him a visa. Graciously, Allah favored him with the opportunity of sowing the seed of Ahmadiyyat in New Zealand. The Ahmadiyya Muslim Community (AMC) in New Zealand is largely comprised of Fiji Ahmadies who had been immigrating to the beautiful South Pacific Country for several decades for education and jobs but in larger numbers after the first military coup in Fiji in 1987. The sons and daughters of Late Lala Mohammed Sidique Khan who knew Dr. Dard very well are now members of the AMC, New Zealand. His sojourn from Fiji to New Zealand, Australia and onward to England has interesting details regarding people of Fiji and numerous personalities he worked closely with and depicted in several photographs that Mr. Dard has wisely inserted at appropriate places in the book. Photos with late Sir Muhammad Zafrullah Khan, and all the Khalifas of Jamaat Ahmadiyya featured in the book unfold a story in themselves.

Mr. Dard's passion for Urdu poetry (sher-o-shairee) was very much talked about when we were his student at the Lautoka Muslim High School in Fiji. His friendship with a fellow teacher Master Hari Prasad- one of Fiji's top ghazal singers, was further evidence of Mr. Dard's love for Urdu that he shared with his friend. I was pleasantly surprised to learn that Mr. Dard would read Urdu shairee for my late uncle Hon. S M Koya a long time Leader of Opposition in the Sir Ratu Mara Government.

Mr. Dard's love for Urdu, inevitably is deeply rooted both in his own family of great servants of Ahmadiyyat and profusely exhibited in his services as the editor Al Manar

In his autobiography, Mr. Dard captures fond memories of his childhood days tracing his ancestry to the chosen 313 companions of the Promised Messiah among whom his grandfather Hazrat Master Qadir Bakhsh of Ludhiana was a key follower of our beloved Imam Hazrat Mirza Ghulam Ahmad, the Promised Messiah and Mehdi (peace be upon him). Given his ancestral background and close affinity with Hazrat Masih-e-Maoud, Mr. Dard enjoyed a close and fond association with the all the Khalifas of the Jamaat all of whom seem to have given some degree of responsibility and regard for his bond and a cheerful spirit for serving Ahmadiyyat the True Islam. As I am writing these few lines and sharing the piece with Mr. Dard via email and phone contact in London, England, Dr. Dard is featured with Hazrat Khalifatul Masih V in English program on MTA- the only 24 Hour Muslim Television, Ahmadiyya, telecast from MTA studios in London.

Mr. Dard ably captures the political manoeuvres of Pakistani governments specially the Zia regime which sought to destroy Jamaat Ahmadiyya but instead Zia met with a tragic death.

The book is a must specially for those who would like to have a peak into the origin of Jamaat Ahmadiyya in Fiji which lies at the very end of the globe, where it is said the day begins because the international dateline that cuts across a major Taveuni Island, thus fulfilling a most important prophecy of Hazrat Masih-e-Maoud (as) " I shall cause thy movement to reach the corners of the earth."

It is a magnificent sign of Allah that Mr. Dard and late Maulana Sheikh Abdul Wahid Fazil have had a significant part in the fulfillment of the grand prophecy.

My fervent prayers are for Mr. Dard for the wonderful service he has rendered as a sincerest Ahmadi Muslim and a deeply dedicated educator. May Allah reward him immensely. Ameen !

Dr Hanif Koya
Superior Court of Alameda
California, USA
Drhkoya@hotmail.com
www.fijisun-usa.com

Early Life 1934-1960

I was born at Qadian, in India, on the 9th September 1934. My father "Haji" Barkatullah was a son of Hadhrat Master Qadir Bakhsh of Ludhiana - one of the three hundred and thirteen chosen companions of the Promised Messiah. He was mentioned as one of the prominent persons of Ludhiana in the book Izala-e-Auhaam written by the Promised Messiah and published in 1891.

Hadhrat Master Qadir Bakhsh (ra)
one of the 313 Companions of the
Promised Messiah (as)

**Standing L to R Musleh Uldin Saadi,
(Haji) Barkart Ullah &
Sitting Hadhrat Mulana Abdul Raheem Dard** (ra)

My mother, Asghari Begum, was a daughter of Dr. Lal Din of Noor Hospital, Qadian. She was born at Hoshiarpur where the Promised Messiah had spent forty days in solitude in 1886. There he was granted an audience with the Supreme Sovereign, and was given the glad tidings of Musleh Maud (Promised Reformer). Hadhrat Ahmad left Qadian for Hoshiarpur on January 20th or 21st, 1886 in a bullock-driven carriage. He was accompanied by Mian Abdullah Sanauri, Sheikh Hamid Ali and Fateh khan. While, they were crossing the river

An Ahmadiyya Muslim

Beas, in an old fashioned boat, Hadhrat Ahmad is reported to have remarked that the company of a holy man is like journeying across a river; there was the hope of landing safely on the other side, but there was also the danger of being drowned. It proved a prophetic remark for one of his three companions, namely Fated Khan deserted him afterwards and was thus spiritually drowned. Hadhrat Ahmad reached Hoshiarpur on Friday January 22nd, 1886. Hadhrat Ahmad occupied the upper story of the house of Sheikh Mehr Ali a leading Muslim of Hoshiarpur. The house was known as his Tavela on the outskirts of the town. Hadhrat Ahmad entrusted different duties to his three companions. My granduncle Mian Abdullah Sanauri was to prepare food for Hadhrat Ahmad and serve it. Sheikh Hamid Ali had to do the house work and also attend to visitors. Fateh Khan was required to do shopping . Strict orders were given by Hadhrat Ahmad to always keep the front door bolted and that no one should disturb him. No one was allowed to go upstairs or to talk to him more than was necessary during the forty days of prayer and meditation. He wanted his meals left upstairs, no one was to wait upon him and the dishes and utensils were to be cleared when he had finished. His instructions were carefully carried out and he was left undisturbed with God.

No one knows what Hadhrat Ahmad did upstairs. Mian Abdullah Sanauri used to take his food to him; and he says that once or twice Hadhrat Ahmad told him a little of the religious experience he was going through. Hadhrat Ahmad was enjoying communion with the Almighty, Who would talk to him for a long time. Hadhrat Ahmad held a long discourse with his Heavenly Father and experienced His love and affection. His experiences were of a nature too deep and intimate to be disclosed to the outside world. He told Hadhrat Mian Abdullah Sanauri that God had revealed to him the following words: "Blessed is the one in it and blessed are those who are around it." He explained its meaning by saying that the first part referred to his own self and the second to his companions present there at that moment. Fateh Khan was absent at the time on an errand.

In view of the subsequent events of Hadhrat Abmad's life, the "Chilla" (forty days of prayers and meditation) appear to have been a preparation and a prelude to his official inauguration as God's ambassador to the world. His credentials were prepared and he was given, as it were, an audience with the Supreme Sovereign. The mighty sign which Hadhrat Ahmad asked of God was also granted him; and it was broadcast by means of a leaflet issued on February 20th, 1886. The prophetic words about the Promised Son (Musleh Maud) were written in the Promised Messiah's own writing at Hoshiarpur and published in the form of an announcement as a supplement to Riyaz Hind. (Amritsar) in its edition of 1st, March 1886.

I lived with my grandmother at the house of my uncle Hadhrat Maulana Abdul -Rahim Dard, in Dar-ul-Anwar, Qadian . I was very fond of calling "Adhan" in

the small Mosque where we all prayed. I vividly remember doing "Waqar-e-Amal" with Hadhrat Khalifatul Masih II in the early 1940s near his house called Dar-ul-Hamd. As a little boy, I filled his basket with soil and generally just hovered around him with the other children. I became a student at Talim-ul-Islam school, living in the boarding house near the Noor Mosque. I recall going for my Fajr Prayers wrapped in a quilt because of the cold. I spent most of my childhood at Dalhousie Hill Station, where my father worked as a sub post-master until 1947. Hadhrat Musleh Maud used to spend some summer months in Dalhousie. He had two houses there at Bakrota called "Bait-ul-Fazl" and "Peace". He used to invite us on Eid day for a meal. I often telephoned him asking about my father if he was late coming home.

Hadhrat Musleh Maoo'd at the wedding of
Maulana Muhammed Shafi Ashraf at Rabwah 1958

(L to R) (Haji) Barakat Ullah, G. M. Akhtar, Rafiullah & Hadhrat Musleh Maoo'd (ra) 1958

I remember Raja Mohammed Nawaz and Mr. Nayk Mohammed Khan who looked after his houses. I also remember that Hadhrat Amma Jaan, wife of the Promised Messiah, often visited our house accompanied by Sahibzadi Amtul Jameel. Hadhrat Amma Jaan helped my mother in preparing and cooking food in the kitchen, while we played, running around as most children do. Hadhrat Amma Jaan treated both my parents very kindly and brought gifts for them. I consider myself extremely fortunate to have been cared for and fed by her for a short time. she frequently visited our house because there was no other Ahmadi family living in Dalhousie. She used to come sitting in a 'Dandy' slung from bamboo poles, carried shoulder-high by two or more men, a common means of transport in hilly districts.

Hardhat Amma Jaan passed away in April, 1952 at Rabwah. I attended her funeral. After a few weeks my mother also died in pregnancy on the last day of the holy month of Ramadan. Inna Lillahe wa inna illahe rajeyoon. (We all belong to Allah, and to him is our return) May Allah grant both of them a lofty station in Paradise. Amin.

Once at Raten Bagh my uncle Hadhrat Maulana A. R. Dard presented me before Hadhrat Musleh Maud. He looked at me fixedly and said, "You used to cry on the road in Dalhousie." He had a fantastic memory. It was during one of his evening walks that I had been crying because someone would not let me walk beside him, and I was lagging behind. Hadhrat Maulana Ghulam Rasool Rajeki and a group of young Missionaries, who were going abroad to preach Islam in Europe, spent a few weeks at Dalhousie Hill station. They all lived near our house. It was my duty to bring hot cups of tea to Hadhrat Maulana Ghulam Rasool Rajeki. I still see him in my mind wrapped in a blanket sitting near my father sipping tea. 1 was about ten years old at the time. The young missionaries held meetings, and I used to collect wild flowers to put on the table. I remember Hafiz Qudratullah, Chaudhary Khalil Ahmad Nasir, Chaudhary Mushtaq Ahmad Bajwa, Chaudhary Zahoor Ahmad Bajwa and Mrs. Kalsoom Mushtaq Bajwa treated me very affectionately.

We emigrated from Dalhousie to Lahore in the company of Hadhrat Nawab Muhammad Din who was a retired deputy commissioner, under the protection of Captain Attaullah. The first time I saw Molvi Muhammad Ali, he was sitting on a stone stair waiting for his transport to arrive. He was the President of the Anjuman Ahmadiyya of Lahore. My father, with his family, was waiting on the verandah of the main post office of Dalhousie on the day of our departure. We were hungry and thirsty on the way; there were riots and refugees were being killed. We were escaping from the murder, looting, rape, and abduction of women, which followed the partition of the subcontinent into India and Pakistan. We reached Lahore safely in August 1947.

On the 31st August 1947 I was present at 13, Temple Road, Lahore, at the house of Sheikh Bashir Ahmad advocate, when Hadhrat Mirza Bashir-ud-Din Mahmood Ahmad Khalifatul Masih II arrived in the afternoon from Qadian. This migration was an historic occasion. I remember that it was decided that his arrival in Lahore would remain a secret for the moment. All present took an oath that no one would reveal this secret until the official announcement of Hazur's arrival. We were living in the house of my uncle Mr. Musleh-ul-Din Saadi with the family of Mr. Noor-ul-Din Jahangir who was working as a food inspector. Mr. Jahangir had seen Hadhrat Musleh Maud travelling in a car fleetingly by chance, but he was not sure about it. On reaching home he asked us whether Hazur had arrived in Lahore or not. My father and I had made an oath not to disclose this information. So we did our best to ignore his questioning. Within a day or two Hazur's migration to Lahore was an open secret. We apologised to Mr. Jahangir for avoiding his questioning.

Hadhrat Musleh Maud took up residence at 'Rattan Bagh' and we moved to 4 McLeod Road, Lahore. After a few months my father was posted as a sub-post master at Samundri.

In 1949 Rabwah town was established in 'mud brick houses', and the Government decided to open a post office there. No non-Ahmadi postal worker was prepared to go to Rabwah because of the harsh conditions. My father offered his services, and was appointed the first sub-post master of Rabwah. We moved from Smaundri to Rabwah. I became a student at the Talim-ul-Islam High School at Chiniot. Hadhrat Syed Mahmud Ullah shah Sahib the headmaster treated me extremely kindly. I passed my Matriculation examination in 1951.

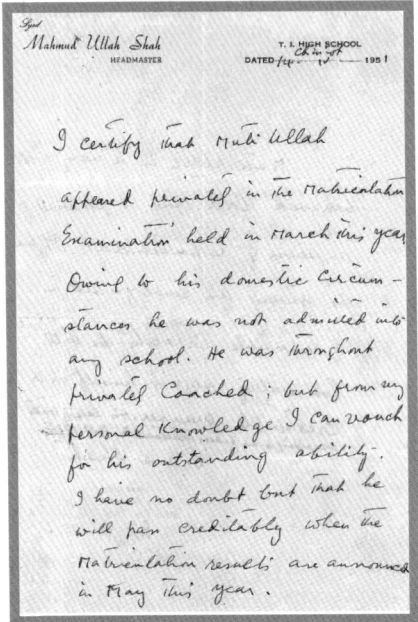 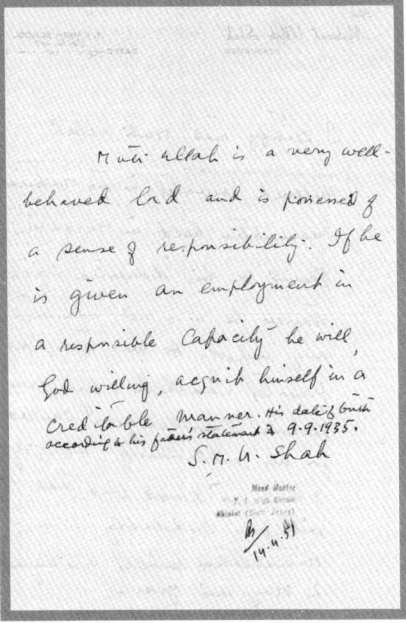

My uncle, Hadhrat Maulana A. R. Dard treated me like his son, and I started living with him. Hadhrat Mirza Aziz Ahmad got me admitted into the Talim- ul-Islam college in Lahore. Hadhrat Mirza Nasir Ahmad the principal, had known me from my early childhood days at Dar-ul-Anwar in Qadian. Once or twice he had very affectionately corrected my mischievous behaviour.

He kept me under his wing, and monitored my educational progress. My uncle Hadhrat Maulana A. R. Dard once asked him about my studies, "He achieves the minimum required" was the reply. But it was by his guidance and help that I sailed through the vicissitudes of student life.

An Ahmadiyya Muslim

The Ahmadiyya Intercollegiate Association held declamation contests. I took part in one of them, and won a second prize, while the first prize was won by Mr. Bashir Ahmad Rafiq at Talim-ul-Islam College Lahore. l passed my F. A. exam in 1953. By 1954 I had become a debater, and was appointed Editor-in-chief of the college magazine "Almanar" . Urdu section for two years.

Abdullah Usman Omer and I represented Talim-ul-Islam college in the All Pakistan Liaqat Memorial Debate at the Government College Quetta in 1953 Our speeches won the first prize in the Urdu debate. Chaudhary Muhammad Ali, Sheikh Mehboob, Alam Khalid, Mr. Abbas Bin Abdul Qadir, Maulana Arjumand Khan, Maulana Ghulam Ahmad Badomalhi Sahib and Akhwand Abdul Kadir Sahib taught and kindly guided me for four years at the College. I was elected as the Vice- President of the Psychological society and the Vice-President of Bazm-e-Urdu in 1954-1955.

Matiullah Dard & Abdullah Osman Omar

Matiullah Dard receiving a prize from Sir Muhammad Zafarullah Khan T I College Lahore 1954

I remember Sir Muhammad Zafrullah Khan, the then Foreign Minister of Pakistan, addressed us in 1954 and I received a prize from him. The college was moved to Rabwah in late l 954. I was one of the nine first graduates who passed from the T. I. College at Rabwah in 1955.

Hadhrat Dr. Mufti Muhammad Sadiq used to come to the post office to collect his mail. Many people wrote to him for prayers. On some occasions it was my good fortune to act as his secretary and wrote the replies. Hadhrat Dr. Mufti Mohammad Sadiq was one of the 313 companions of the Promised Messiah, and was the prominent private secretary to the Promised Messiah. He was an undergraduate when he dedicated his life to serve Ahmadiyyat at the wish of the Promised Messiah. Allah later blessed him with a couple of honorary doctorate

An Ahmadiyya Muslim

degrees in the USA. The Promised Messiah had said "degrees would come later - you come now and serve Islam" What a prophetic utterance!

M. A. Psychology Final year students & staff at Govt. College Lahore 1957

I moved to Lahore and joined the Islamia College for an MA degree in Psychology. Dr. Saeedullah, head of the Psychology Department knew that I was an Ahmadi. He told me that he went to Qadian along with Dr. Sir Muhammad Iqbal and Saifuddeen Kitchloo for Bai'at at the hands of Hadhrat Masih Maoud Alaihissalam and was also a regular subscriber to Daily Al-Fazl newspaper. After a few months I migrated to the Government college at Lahore. I passed my MA degree in 1958 from the Punjab University while I was working as a Social Education -cum - Public Relations officer in Sargodha.

My uncle Hadhrat Maulana A R. Dard died in December 1955. Many members of our family offered their services for the cause of Islam. I had also offered. I was asked by Hadhrat Khalifatul Masih II to resign my post at Sargodha and come to Rabwah. I did so. Hadhrat Mirza Bashir-ul-Din Mahmood Ahmad Khalifatul Masih Sani appointed me as a Naib Nazir and gave me instructions on how to assist Hadhrat Waliullah Shah Sahib, who was then Nazir Amoor-e-Kharja.

In fact, Hazur had a dream that he was looking for a substitute for A. R. Dard Sahib. He met his younger brother Mirza Bashir Ahmad and said to him that the name of Soofi Abdul-Qadeer Niaz came to his mind. Hazur informed Hadhrat Mirza Bashir Ahmad about his dream, and he in turn wrote to Soofi A. Q. Niaz about it. In response Soofi A. Q. Niaz offered himself without hesitation or any conditions. Hadhrat Soofi A.Q. Naiz had retired after a long, distinguished and dedicated service to the Ahmadiyya Movement. He was also the first missionary and founder of the Ahmadiyya Muslim Movement in Japan in 1935. When I met Hazur at Rabwah he appointed me to work with the Nazir Amoor-e-Kharja, he

An Ahmadiyya Muslim 16

said that he had had an intimation and thought that it referred to Habib-ul-Rehman Dard (son of uncle Dard) but he was still studying. It is my understanding that he applied his divine intimation to me, and appointed me instead.

Before I was given charge of my new appointment the then Nazir-e-Diwan had proposed a training programme for me. I was directed to spend six month in every Nazarat. I spent the first six months in Nazarate-Ulia where my benefactor Hadhrat Mirza Aziz Ahmad Sahib was Nazire-Alla. In the seventh month I went to Nazarate-Bait-ul-Mal. Mr. Abdus-Salam Akhtar, a Naib Nazir, helped me to understand financial matters. I remember that Hadhrat Mirza Bashir Ahmad Sahib took a very keen interest in my training. He used to ask me, almost daily, about my work before our Maghrib prayer in Masjid Mubarak while pacing up and down. He talked about my case with Hadhrat Mirza Nasir Ahmad who was the President of Sadr Anjuman Ahmadiyya.

 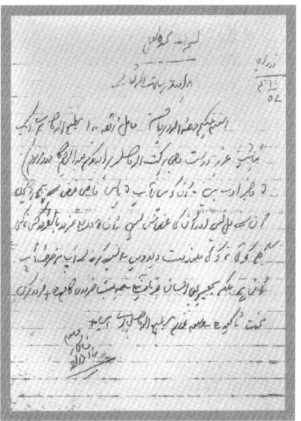

My uncle Hadhrat Chaudhary Fateh Muhammad Sayyal and Hadhrat Mian Sharif Ahmad also took an interest in my case. I was living with Hadhrat F. M. Sayyal in his house at the time. He said to me that they had been thinking about making a proposal in a meeting of the Sadr-Anjuman Ahmadiyya, that I should be sent abroad as a missionary. Hadhrat F. M. Sayyal died in 1960. I attended him all night. Hadhrat Mirza Bashir Ahmad asked me to report to him hourly about his condition which was deteriorating . I did this easily because Hadhrat Mian Bashir Ahmad was the next door neighbour.

Hadhrat F. M. Sayyal passed away in the morning . Chaudhary Nasir Muhammad Sayyal his son arrived just before his death. Hadhrat Fateh Muhammad Sayyal was the first missionary and founder of the Ahmadiyya Muslim Mission in the United Kingdom.

Matiullah Dard, Hadhrat Maulana Ghulam Rasool Rajeki (ra) & Rafiullah

Matiullah Dard as Naib Nazir (Deputy Director) Sadr Anjuman Ahmadiyya Rabwah 1959

Ahmadiyya Mission-Fiji

In 1959 an elderly gentleman, Haji Muhammad Ramzan Khan of Fiji visited Rabwah. He was researching the facts about the institution of the Khilafat-e-Ahmadiyya. Hadhrat Khalifatul Masih II had been trying to open an Ahmadiyya Mission in Fiji.
Hadhrat Mirza Mubarak Ahmad Vakeel-ul-Tabsheer acquired my services from Sadr Anjuman Ahmadiyya and asked me to persuade Haji Ramzan Khan Sahib to join the Khilafat-e-Ahmadiyya. Sheikh Abdul Wahid missionary designate for Fiji and I spent quite a bit of time convincing him about the institution of the Khilafat. He was very reluctant to accept, but Sheikh Sahib and I eventually succeeded to bring him around to our way of thinking. He joined the Jama'at at Rabwah. His daughter Bader-ul-Nisa was married to my cousin sheikh Anwar Rasool. Hadhrat Mirza Bashir-ul-Din Mahmood Ahmad, Khalifatul Masih II, had expressed the wish, regarding this marriage, that it might pave the way for establishing the Ahmadiyya Mission in Fiji. It came true. When, Haji Ramzan Khan came to meet his daughter in Lahore after pilgrimage in Saudi Arabia in 1959. It was decided that I should marry his granddaughter. Hadhrat Maulana Jalal-ul-Din Shams announced my Nikah with the permission of Hadhrat Khalifatul Masih II on the 20th January 1960 in the Mubarak Mosque, Rabwah. Haji Ramzan Khan went back to Fiji. He was able to obtain a permit for Sheikh Abdul Wahid to enter Fiji as a minister of religion, and a permit for me to enter as a teacher. After consulting Hadhrat Mirza Bashir Ahmad and Hadhrat Mirza Nasir Ahmad I requested Hadhrat Khalifatul Masih II to grant me permission to go abroad for higher education.

Hazur kindly allowed me to leave on the condition that Sadr Anjuman Ahmadiyya would not pay for expenses. Sadr Anjuman passed resolution number 1 18 on the 5th March 1960 approving my leave of absence for four years. I requested Hadhrat Maulana Ghulam Rasool Rajeki to pray for me before I left for Fiji. It was his practice that he used to start praying there and then in the meeting. We both raised our hands for prayer. As soon as he finished praying for me he said, "I have seen a light spreading far and wide." Allah gave me the chance to spread the light of Ahmadiyyat in Fiji and New Zealand in fulfillment of the Prophecy of the Promised Messiah that the message of Ahmadiyyat would spread to the corners of the earth.

Sheikh Abdul Wahid, Haji Ramzan Khan & Matiullah Dard at
the Nandi International Airport Fiji 1961

An Ahmadiyya Muslim

Preaching Ahmadiyyat in Fiji & New Zealand 1960-1963

Sheikh Abdul Wahid and I reached Fiji in late 1960. I wholeheartedly joined Sheikh Sahib in preaching activities. We both visited various people's houses regularly, and explained the necessity of the Khilafat. The Ahmadies in Fiji belonged to the Anjuman Ahmadiyya of Maulvi Mohammed Ali of Lahore. Our main task was to convince them with cogent arguments and facts about the institution of Khilafat in Islam, particularly after the demise of the Promised Messiah.

One day early in 1961 Sheikh Abdul Wahid, missionary in charge, decided that I should go to the house of Lala Siddique in Lautoka, and persuade him and his family to join us in the Khilafat-e-Ahmadiyya. All other approaches had been unsuccessful. Sheikh Sahib gave me two initiation forms and said, "I will constantly pray for your success. You go to preach, and bring back at least one form filled in. If they accept, then many others will follow their example." I went to Lala Siddique's house in the morning and spent all day arguing and explaining to them the importance of the institution of the Khilafat-e- Ahmadiyya. Allah blessed him and his wife with understanding, and by the evening, I was eventually able to initiate both of them into the fold of Khilafat-e-Ahmadiyya. Sheikh Sahib was well pleased with the humble efforts of this foot soldier of Ahmadiyyat. Lala Siddique's sons names ended in "Ullah" like my name, Matiullah. They were Khairullah, Zafarullah, Nimatullah and Asmatullah. I suppose "the Ullah brothers" felt a filial affinity with me for the sake of Allah, and soon after, all the sons and daughters of Lala Siddique accepted the Khilafat-e-Ahmadiyya. I was delighted to learn from Sheikh Abdul Wahid's letter to me in 1967, that Lala Siddique was elected as the regional president of Nandi. His wife was appointed president of Lajna Imaillah Fiji.

Matiullah Dard & Lala Siddique Khan & members of Ahmadiyya Jamaat at Lautoka Mosque Fiji 1962

She attended the annual gathering of the Ahmadiyya Muslim Movement at Rabwah in 1973 I also attended the Jalsa, and my cousin Baji Razia Dard met her among the ladies. Slowly but surely Allah blessed our efforts and the majority of Lahori Ahmadies joined us. A mission house was established at Samabula, in Suva, the capital of Fiji. Apart from religious preaching, I was asked to give a talk on Urdu Literature on Radio Fiji. I particularly mentioned Hadhrat Mirza Ghulam Ahmad as "Sultan-ul-Qalam" a prolific religious writer of great merit, noted by the Ulemas of India. The first annual Jalsa of Fijian Ahmadies was held and organised by the Ahmadiyya Muslim mission in Suva on the 29th and 30th December 1962. I delivered a speech on "Ahmadiyyat", which was greatly appreciated by all present.

On the 3rd June 1962, my son Ahmad Krishan Dard was born at the Lautoka hospital. Mr. and Mrs. Lala Siddique and Brethren Khairullah and Nimatullah treated me very affectionately, and helped me tremendously in my hour of need at Lautoka. A few days before my departure from Fiji Sheikh Abdul Wahid, Missionary Incharge informed me that I had been appointed the Auditor for the Tahrik-i- Jadid Anjuman Ahmadiyya-Overseas Mission-Fiji by the Vakeel-ul-Tabsheer, Rabwah.

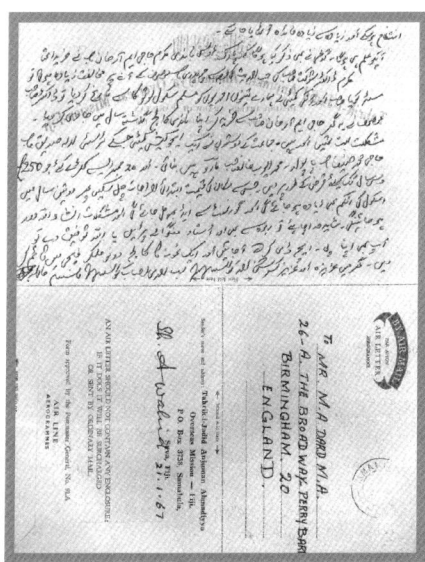
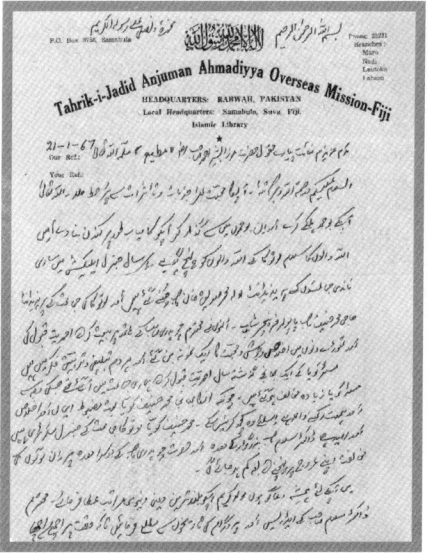

I applied to the Home Office to take up a teaching post in England and was issued with a work permit. On the 21st September 1963 I flew to Auckland, New Zealand. Although my Pakistani passport did not allow me to visit New Zealand, I requested the representative of New Zealand in Fiji to permit me to visit New Zealand. He requested the Government of New Zealand, they accepted his recommendation. I was given a visa for two weeds. I met many Yugoslavian Muslims living in Auckland, and I was given the opportunity to address them in a small meeting. I told them about the Ahmadiyya movement in Islam. I also preached to an Indian Muslim family by the name of Rawat, and they made contact with Rabwah.

It was a sheer blessing of Allah that I became the first preacher of Ahmadiyyat in New Zealand. I stayed at Auckland for ten days. On the 30th September I flew to Sydney, Australia, and visited the capital, Canberra. I stayed with Mr. Sharif Ahmad who was the superintendent in the Pakistan High Commission. I was invited by Dr. Barakat Ahmad of the Indian High Commission for an evening meal, both of these gentlemen were Ahmadies.

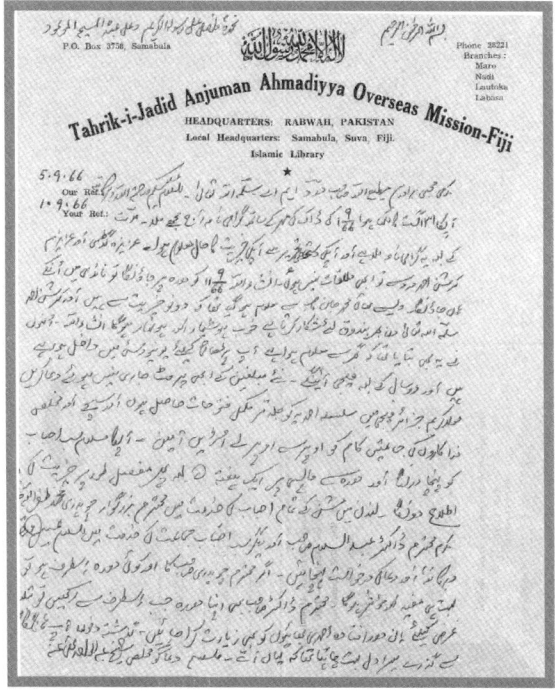

On the 9th October 1963 I boarded the Italian ship TV Roma, Flota Laura at Sydney. The ship went past the Great Barrier Reef and stopped in Singapore for a day. I visited the Ahmadiyya Mission there and met the missionary in charge and signed the visitors book. The next port of call was Bombay. Here again I went to the Ahmadiyya Mission house and met Mr. Yusuf Irfani. I asked him about my long lost cousin Ata-ul-Rehman Dard, who was rumoured to be living in Bombay. Mr. Irfani did not know his whereabouts, and I walked in search of my cousin here, there, and everywhere, hoping that I might meet him by chance, but in vain. I came back to my ship very sad indeed. Once at Qadian I injured my nose because I was being chased by my elder cousin Baji Saliha Dard, and I hit the edge of a table. I was seven or eight years old at the time. I remember that my cousin Ata-ul-Rehman Dard (Bhaijan) kindly used to take me on his bicycle to a dispensary where a "Dr". Ehsan Ali treated my injury. I had remembered Bhaijan with love and affection, and was hoping for a miracle to find him in Bombay. During this voyage I was able to visit the pyramids in Egypt and the Mosque of Sultan Salah-ul-Din Ayyubi in Cairo while my ship went through the Suez Canal. I reached Genoa in Italy on the 8th November, 1963. I boarded a train from Genoa to Paris, and went on to Calais. I reached Dover by ferry en-route to London on the 9th November 1963. In London I stayed with Mr. Eshwary Prasad a dental surgeon, in Woolwich. He was the younger brother of Master Hari Prasad, who was my colleague at the Lautoka Muslim high school where I had taught English to Secondary pupils.

Matiullah Dard with Hadhrat Mirza Waseem Ahmed in Birmingham

Praying in Bait ul Dua at Qadian in 1973

Teaching in Birmingham, England 1964-1999

The day after my arrival, on the 10th November 1963 the first thing I wanted to go and see was the Fazl Mosque. It was a childhood wish of mine to see the First Mosque of London, built in 1924-1926.

My two uncles were both connected with the Mosque. Hadhrat Chaudhary Fateh Muhammad Sayyal bought the land in Putney in 1920, and Hadhrat Maulana Abdul-Rahim Dard supervised the building of the Mosque as its first Imam. My friend Eshwary and I were met by Mr. B. A. Rafiq, the deputy Imam, and I said nafl prayers in the Mosque. I also went to see Professor Abdus- Salam F. R. S. and his most hospitable wife Amtul Hafeez, my "Apa Hafeeza". For my further education Professor Salam suggested that I should go to Cambridge and study. He very kindly said, "Give my name as your referee wherever you apply, and I will highly recommend you."

Eshwary Prasad's friend Miss Moya Saxton was the secretary general of Rotary International. She helped me to obtain recognition for my MA qualification in Psychology from the Department on Education and Science, London. I was given postgraduate qualified teacher status on the basis of my M.A. qualification.

I applied for a teaching post in Birmingham . Professor Salam and Miss Moya Saxton were my referees. Birmingham Local Education Authority offered me a position as a teacher. I started teaching on the 6th April, 1964 at Upper Thomas Street Junior School, Aston.

I taught in various Primary schools in the city until 1984. In 1980 I was appointed as Chairman of the Urdu Language Panel of the City of Birmingham Education Authority. The panel produced four books, and slowly the Urdu language became part of the main curriculum of schools where there was sufficient need, and a demand by the parents. As the demand for, and an educational appreciation of, community languages grew, the City of Birmingham Education Authority promoted me, and appointed me as a Consortium Liaison Linguist between Community Languages and Modem European Languages.

I visited various Secondary schools and colleges to organise and teach Urdu from 1984 to 1987. The Joseph Chamberlain Sixth Form College put me as the lecturer in charge of the Urdu department on a full-time basis in 1987. I taught Urdu to GCSE and A level classes until 1992. After my retirement from the City of

Birmingham I was employed as a part-time lecturer in Urdu by Joseph Chamberlain sixth Form College from January 1993 to April 1999.

After this brief sketch I turn now in some detail to another aspect of my life as a founder member and first nominated Financial Secretary and later on the second elected president of the Ahmadiyya Muslim Community in Birmingham.

DEPARTMENT OF MATHEMATICS
Professor of Applied Mathematics
ABDUS SALAM, Ph.D.

IMPERIAL COLLEGE
SOUTH KENSINGTON,
LONDON - - S.W.7
Telephone: KENSINGTON 5111

March, 1964.

Dear Sir,

I have known in a personal capacity Mr M. Dard for the last 15 years. Mr Dard holds a Master's degree in Psychology from the University of Panjab, Lahore. He is an earnest young man with a pleasing personality, mature and responsible in outlook. He has experience as teacher for 11+'s in Fiji but I have personally not heard him lecture or give lessons. In my opinion he has the making of a fine teacher.

Yours sincerely,
A. Salam

The Early History Of The Ahmadiyya Muslim Movement In Birmingham, UK.

The Ahmadiyya Muslim Community was established in Birmingham in November 1964 in the house of Malik Noor Ahmad at 34, Second Avenue, Selly Park, B29. The Imam of the Fazl Mosque London and Missionary in Charge visited Birmingham to organise the members and nominated Mr. Muhammad Abdul-Rashid and Mr. Matiullah Dard as President and Financial Secretary respectively. There were some other Ahmadies living in and around Birmingham who were contacted and informed about the establishment of the Jama'at.
This news was published in the Daily Al-Fazl and Badr of Qadian.

During 1965/66 community meetings were held at Alcester Road South Birmingham at the house of Mr. Muhammad Idris Chughtai. He was appointed as the General Secretary of the community, and Mr. Abdul Wase Adam Chughtai was appointed as the Publicity Secretary. Sir Muhammad Zafrullah Khan attended one of our monthly meetings and lovingly remembered the ancestors of the Chughtai brothers, Hadhrat Mian Chiragh Din and Hadhrat Hakim Muhammad Hussain Murham Isa of Lahore, during the early years of the Second Khilafat. In 1966/67 many other Ahmadies came to settle in Birmingham. Mr. Rashid Ahmad came from Sierra Leone, and Chaudhary Abdul Hafeez settled here. There were some Ahmadiyya families living at Leamington Spa, Coventry, Walsall and other surrounding areas. They all belonged to the Ahmadiyya Muslim Jamaat of Birmingham. Malik Nisar Ahmad, Syed Zahoor Ahmad Shah, Malik Muhammad Yaqub, Mr. Abdul Hadi Mehta, Mr. Muhammad Afzal Sethi, Sheikh Masood Ahmed, Mr. Mubashar Ahmad Khan, Malik Fazl Ilahi, Malik Abdul Rehman and Malik Mohammad Ahmad had already settled here. The family of the late Mr. Fazal Ilahi bought a house in Halesowen. His widow was a sister of Mr. Bashir Ahmad Hayat of London. Her sons took a keen interest in community affairs. Sir Muhammad Zafrullah Khan treated them affectionately and prayed for them. He was kind to my son Ahmad Krishan Dard, and prayed for him constantly at my earnest request. He was a true servant of Allah. I have been the recipient of his favours and affection on many occasions. He sometimes replied to my letters in his own handwriting in Urdu from the International Court of Justice, Peace Palace, at the Hague.

M. Dard introducing his son Ahmed Krishan Dard to Sir Muhammad Zafarullah Khan

M. Dard, Sir Muhammad Zafarullah Khan, B. A. Rafiq & Ahmed Krishan Dard

Matiullah Dard with Sir Muhammad Zafarullah Khan in London

Mr. Zafar Mahmood dental surgeon had his practice in Solihull. He built a spacious house in Lady Byron Lane, Knowle. Once we had our monthly meeting there. Mrs. Attiyya Zafar proved a great hostess. Once Sir Muhammad Zafrullah Khan and I had a delicious meal cooked by her. Chaudhary Abdul Ghafoor and his brother Mr. Muhammad Rafiq took an active part in preaching activities in Leamington Spa. Mr. Abdul Ghani, the Jeweler, and his sons Munawar Ahmad, Mubashar Ahmad and Muzzaffar Ahmad of Walsall participated in preaching activities with enthusiasm. Mr. Munawar Ahmad published monthly 'Alkhatam' for preaching in later years.

Hadhrat Mirza Mubarak Ahmad Vakeel-ul Tabsheer Tehrik-e-Jadid visited in June 1965 for a day, along with Mir Masood Ahmad and Imam Bashir Ahmad Rafiq, and reviewed the activities of the community as part of his world tour. The distinguished visitors were entertained at my flat. Mr. Muhammad Abdul Rashid and I left no stone unturned to advance the cause of Ahmadiyyat. We went around to various Ahmadiyya houses to collect mandatory and voluntary contributions from the members. The monthly contributions hardly reached above £10.00 Newly arrived immigrants had to face many difficulties in order to settle in the U. K.

Mr. Mohammad Abdul Rashid was a thorough gentleman, kind, honest and a very popular social worker employed in the Pakistan Consulate. When Mr. B. A. Rafiq, the Imam, wanted to nominate and appoint me as the first president, I declined because Mr. MA Rashid had been working and living in the city, and was more familiar with local conditions than me. I had recently arrived here from Fiji, and thought that it would be better for the progress of the Ahmadiyya movement in Birmingham if Mr. MA Rashid was appointed. So I made this suggestion. The Imam agreed. Mr. MA Rashid proved himself worthy of the trust. He had a mini car that was used for community purposes. I remember that he visited me in Dudley Road Hospital, where I was having a minor operation, every day for a week he looked after my family like a true brother. May Allah bless him and his family always. Ameen.

In early 1967 he left Birmingham and settled in North London. He has been President of the North London Jama'at, and an active member in the Central Ahmadiyya Association UK for many years. Allah has blessed him and his wife "Bhabi Fahmeeda" with his two daughters, Dr. Sultana and Shazia and two sons Dr. Shah Nawaz and Qudsy. When Mr. Muhammad Abdul Rashid left Birmingham for London, the financial secretary was approved as an Acting President by the Imam and missionary in Charge of the U. K.

The membership of the Birmingham Community increased with the arrival of immigrants from Asian and African countries. Mr. Muhammad Iqbal Dar and his brother Mr. Muhammad Ikram Dar came from Tanzania. In 1964 when

Tanganyika and Zanzibar were merged Mr. Muhammad Iqbal Dar entered an international competition to name the new East African country.
The competition involved eighty eight different countries and Mr. Muhammad Iqbal Dar's winning effort Tanzania. earned him a national medal, a certificate and a small amount of money.

Mr. Qari Muhammad Yasin Khan's son Muhammad Ilyas Khan, a young trainee barrister, came here to work. I was requested by his father to look after young Ilyas and encourage him to become an active member of the community. He became the General Secretary later in 1970. After a few years he was elected as the President of the Ahmadiyya Muslim community, Birmingham. I have continually prayed for him that Allah might honour him and appoint him eventually as a judge of the British High Court. Amin. (He is now a Recorder.)

The first proper election was held according to the rules of the community on the 3rd December, 1967. The following office bearers were elected and approved by the Imam and Missionary in Charge of the United Kingdom.

President	Mr. Matiullah Dard
General & Financial Secretary	Chaudhary Abdul Hafeez
Education Secretary	Mr. Rashid Ahmad

My house at 50 The Broadway, Birmingham, B20 3EA was declared as the Centre of the Ahmadiyya Muslim Community. The front room of this house was set apart for community activities and as an Advice Bureau. The monthly meetings were held regularly at various Ahmadi members houses in turn.

It became obvious that we should have a larger place for our monthly meetings in order to meet the growing needs of the community. We hired a big room at the Newtown Community Centre in Lozells, for this purpose every month for a few hours. A separate room was hired for ladies meetings. It was decided that we should hold our monthly meetings on the first Sunday of every month. This practice is still followed.
Mr. Rashid Ahmad conducted education classes for children. Mr. Abdul Rashid Arshad Rehan assisted the Education Secretary.

In 1967, Hadhrat Molvi Qudratullah Sanauri and Sheikh Mubarak Ahmad, Secretary of the Fazle-Umer Foundation visited Birmingham to collect donations for the Fazle-Umer. Foundation. Most members participated in the scheme willingly and generously.

In 1968 Dr. Nazir Ahmad arrived to live and work in Birmingham. He enjoyed the kind hospitality of Chaudhary Abdul Hafeez for about four months at 50, Warren Road, before starting his general practice at 1 Witton Road, Aston. Dr. Nazir Ahmad was an enthusiastic preacher and became the instrument of converting a number of West Indian people. Mr. Shakeel Ahmad, computer programmer, worked as the secretary Tehrik-e Jadid for some months. He moved to London in 1969. The Juma prayers were held at the Ahmadiyya Muslim Centre and Dr. Nazir Ahmad's surgery.

In 1970, Dr. Syed Farooq Ahmad was working in the Manor Hospital, Walsall. One day he started proselytizing another doctor called Muhammad Zakariya Tahir. Dr. Muhammad Zakariya Tahir was an Ahmadi from Pakistan, but Syed Farooq Ahmad did not know that because Dr. Syed Farooq Ahmad had recently come from Bihar in India. After listening for quite a while, Dr. Tahir smiled and without saying a word went away. Dr. Syed Farooq Ahmad telephoned me and reported his zealous preaching. As soon as he mentioned the name of Dr. Zakariya Tahir I surprised him by saying that Dr. M. Z. Tahir was already an Ahmadi. Dr. Farooq apologized to Dr. Tahir, and later on both became partners in general practice.

On the 20th August 1970 the famous poet Mr. Saqib Zeervi along with Chaudhary Muhammad Idris Nasrullah Khan, Chaudhary Hidaitullah Bangvi and Imam Bashir Ahmad Rafiq visited the Ahmadiyya Muslim Centre, Birmingham. I took Mr. Saqib Zeervi to the BBC Television Studios where some of his poems were recorded by Mr. Salim Shahid of the BBC Asian programme. Later that evening I took him and Chaudhary Idris Nasrullah Khan to Coventry. Before he left Mr. Saqib Zeervi recited some of his poems in his melodious voice to entertain us at my house.

Sahibzada M. M. Ahmad & Matiullah Dard at Ahmad Salam's wedding in London

Sahibzada Mirza Mansoor Ahmad & Matiullah Dard in Birmingham

The Dream

I would like to mention one of the dreams I had as a special bounty of Allah. I had the following dream before I became a vehicle of converting a few English people to Ahmadiyyat in early 1971.

I ran up stairs made of cement and reached a door, which opened suddenly in front of me. Inside the room, in the centre, sat an elderly woman wearing a pure white dress emitting effulgent light, which filled the room. I was dazzled by the richness of the light. She held me and put my head on her thigh as a mother caresses a child. After a few minutes I woke up form this dream. Its effulgence is stamped on my heart and mind as an ever fresh memory forever.

I mentioned this dream to Hadhrat Maulana Abdul Malik Nazir Islah-O-Irshad when I was driving him, his wife and a daughter in my car from Birmingham to the American Embassy in London. I also interpreted my dream in a way that it was a glad tiding from Allah that if I remained a good Ahmadi Muslim, Allah out of His infinite mercy and forgiveness would grant me salvation in the hereafter.

This was the first interpretation which came to my mind. There were other interpretations as well, but my heart and mind did not, and would not, accept them. After listening to my narration and questioning some details of the dream Hadhrat Maulana Abdul Malik agreed with my first interpretation, but only Allah knows the true significance of this dream. A disobedient sinner like me most certainly does not deserve salvation on merit.

Allah's mercy is boundless, and I hope that His compassion and forgiveness would cover my sins and blunders. This is the only hope of salvation I do entertain in my heart and mind and nothing else of my actions can save me!

There is no need of witnesses,
I confess most humbly, O Lord
I Indeed am a sinner!
I beseech you, O my Lord
Turn to mercy, please
And cover my blunders - with your
Encompassing forgiveness
And ignore my faults!!
Amin

Ahmadiyya Preaching Progress

In order to meet our preaching needs, and to introduce the Ahmadiyya Muslims the following measure were taken:
1. The Ahmadiyya Muslim Centre was put in the telephone directory and the 'People to People' directory published by the Community Relations Committee of the City of Birmingham.
2. The Year Book' of the city of Birmingham included the name and address of the Ahmadiyya Muslim Centre.
3. Seventeen volumes of Rohani Khazain by the Promised Messiah and five volumes of the English translation and commentary of the Holy Quran by Hadhrat Mirza Bashir-ul-Din Mahmood Ahmad were bought by the city of Birmingham Reference Library. Many other books on Islam and Ahmadiyyat were donated to the Central Library, schools, colleges, universities and other libraries in various parts of the city.
4. SHAP Working Party on World Religions in Education. The Junior Sub-Group U. K. appointed me as a member in 1971. They held their meetings in London. This opportunity was fully exploited and the famous book by the Promised Messiah .The Philosophy of the Teachings of Islam" was distributed to teachers and members. The book was also freely given as a gift to all members of Theology at a two day Religious Conference at Regent's Park College, Oxford in 1972.

Here I met Sahibzada Mirza Anas Ahmad, who was studying at Oxford University for a B. Litt. Degree. He very kindly accepted my invitation and spent many of his holidays with me in Birmingham.

Sahibzada Mirza Anas Ahmad & Matiullah Dard at Birmingham & Stratford upon Avon

An Ahmadiyya Muslim

Mr. Neville Ward and his fiancee, Miss Valerie Miles were young teachers in their early twenties. Mr. Ward and I were colleagues at a primary school in Handsworth. I started preaching Islam to the young couple. Mr. Ward mentioned his constant nightmare - a lion frightened him and drove him to hide in a cave in his dreams. I explained the Islamic interpretation of dreams and said that if he became an Ahmadiyya Muslim the nightmare would disappear Inshallah, forever. He read the Holy Quran and some other books. Apart from preaching to him and his fiancee, I taught them how to cook curries with Halal meat. They surprised me one day, and became Ahmadi Muslims with understanding. Hadhrat Mirza Nasir Ahmad Khalifatul Masih III gave them Islamic names. Neville was named Nasir Wasim Ward and Valerie was named Waliyya Qudsiyya. Their Muslim marriage was solemnized at the Fazl Mosque, London. They were probably the first English Muslim couple whose marriage was celebrated at the mosque. The Ahmadiyya bulletin dated August 1971 reported their conversion into Ahmadiyyat. Midland BBC Television interviewed Mr. Nasir Ward because he had accepted Islam. Mr. Ward explained the reasons for his conversion to Islam. For a short time Mr. Nasir Ward was General Secretary of the community before he moved to Slough. Dr. Nazir Ahmad and his German wife Khadijah played a significant role in instructing and educating the newlywed English couple, Mr. & Mrs. Ward. I also converted a Turkish student Mr. Durran Tekin from Anatolia into Ahmadiyyat. The successful preaching activities impressed Sir Muhammad Zafrullah Khan so much that he came from the Hague to Birmingham, and spent a full day with the new converts at Dr. Nazir Ahmad's surgery at 1, Witton Road, Aston.

Hadhrat Mirza Nasir Ahmad Kahlifatul Masih III & Matiullah Dard in London

Nasir Ward, Durran Tekin, Matiullah Dard, Sir M. Zafarullah Kan & Saleem Siddiqi

An Ahmadiyya Muslim 34

On the 19th August 1970 Miss Naeema Dard, daughter of Hadhrat Maulana A. R. Dard the first Imam of the London Mosque was married to Dr. Rab Nawaz of the U.S.A. He came from Wisconsin to Birmingham to take his bride away. The Nikah was announced by Hadhrat Mirza Nasir Ahmad Khalifatul Masih III in Rabwah. My cousin Naeema had arrived a few days earlier from Pakistan. Dr. Nazir Ahmad led the prayers to conclude the Rukhstana Ceremony at the Ahmadiyya Muslim Centre. After a few days the newlywed couple flew away to the USA Dr. Rab Nawab was a professor at the University of Wisconsin, USA.

I would like to thank Chaudhary Abdul Hafeez, the General Secretary, for recording the minutes of our monthly meetings from 5th May 1968 to 6th October 1968. A new General secretary, Mr. Muhammad Ilyas Khan was appointed for a few months. He recorded the minutes of the two meetings held on the 5th April and the 3rd May 1970. Mr. Rashid Ahmad. Secretary Education, recorded the minutes of the monthly meetings of June and July 1970. He also recorded the details of the special monthly meeting held on the 1st November 1970, in which Sahibzada Mirza Anas Ahmad addressed the community on the basic concept of God Almighty at the Ahmadiyya Muslim Centre. He exhorted us to read the Holy Quran with understanding daily, and also to read the books of the Promised Messiah.

Durran Tekin, Nasir Ward, Bashir Ahmad Orchard & Matiullah Dard

The Eighth Annual Conference of the Ahmadiyya Muslim Movement in Great Britain was held on the 28th and 29th August 1971 at Mahmud Hall, the London Mosque. At the ladies conference Mrs. Khadeja Nazir spoke on "How I accepted Islam". Mr. Matiullah Dard read some quotations, and Dr. Nazir Ahmad addressed the conference on 'techniques of preaching, While Mr. Muhammad Idris Chughtai recited a portion of the Holy Quran. 'The Imam, Mr. Sharif Ahmad Bajwa greatly appreciated the effort of the Birmingham Community. A group photograph of the English and other new converts was taken with the Imam and Missionary in Charge, Mr. S. A. Bajwa.

On the 5th September 1971 in our monthly meeting held at Mr. Adam Chughtai's house, Mr. Nasir Ward and Mr. Durran Tekin were introduced to the community. Both gentlemen had recently accepted Ahmadiyyat. Mr. D. Tekin explained why he had become an Ahmadi Muslim.

L to R. N. Scrivener, M. Clarke, A. Ghauri, A. M. Rashid, N. Ward, M. Dard, S. A. Bajwa (Iman), D. Tekin, B. Orchard at Fazl Mosque

On the 3rd October, 1971, in the monthly meeting, again at Mr. Adam Chughtai's house, Mr. Nasir ward was requested to speak on how and why he became an Ahmadi. First of all Mr. Ward thanked Mr. Dard, through whom the message of Islam & Ahmadiyyat had reached him, then he explained the beauties of Islamic teachings. At the end of his speech he also answered many questions put to him by the Ahmadi brethren. Mr. Rashid Ahmad recorded the minutes of these meetings. He was appointed the General Secretary as well as Education Secretary.

In 1971, Lajna Imaillah was established. Mrs. Bushra Kishwar, wife of Mr. Abdul Wasi Adam Chughtai and Mrs. Waliyya Quadsiyya, wife of Mr. Nasir Wasim Ward were nominated as the first President and secretary respectively. This was approved by the President of the U. K. Lajna Imaillah. Mrs. Amtul Hafeez Begum, wife of Dr. A. Salam, the Nobel Laureate in Physics.

I was elected as the first representative of the Pakistani Community on the City of Birmingham Community Relations Council for three years from 1972 to 1975. I also distributed the book 'The Philosophy of the Teachings of Islam" to the council members, and kept on urging the council to appoint members of other religions apart from Christian clergy. The council agreed. A list of organisations where

Pakistani citizens could apply for information and advice free of charge was published and distributed extensively in the libraries and through other channels. Our address was published at the top of the list by the Community Relations Council of the city. This was a good introduction for the Ahmadiyya Muslim Community. In short, every avenue was explored and utilized to make the Ahmadiyya movement known to people in general.

Sir Muhammad Zafarullah Khan with members of Birmingham Jamaat at Halesowen 1972

Bashir Rafiq (Imam London Mosque)
delivering a speech

A special meeting was held on the 3rd June 1972 at 31 Springfield Road, Kings Heath, the home of Mr. Abdul Wase Adam Chughtai. The Imam, Mr. B. A. Rafiq and Sir Muhammad Zafrullah Khan, President of the International Court of Justice, addressed the community members and reviewed the activities of the community. I presented the progress report since November 1964. I particularly appreciated the work done by all the secretaries and thanked them all. Sir Muhammad Zafrullah Khan had expressed his delight at the progress of the Community in Birmingham in a letter to me in May 1972.

He wanted to visit to encourage us all to propagate Ahmadiyyat by giving us advice and guidance. May Allah bless him and exalt his station in paradise. Amin.

COUR INTERNATIONALE DE JUSTICE — INTERNATIONAL COURT OF JUSTICE
PALAIS DE LA PAIX, LA HAYE, PAYS-BAS — PEACE PALACE, THE HAGUE, NETHERLANDS

10 May 1972

Dear Mr. Dard,

Many thanks for your letter of April 21 of which I have noted the contents. I shall be very happy to furnish a reference if and when an enquiry is made from me. I have so far not received the particular reference which you have mentioned in your letter.

I am delighted to learn of the progress that the Community is making in Birmingham. I was in London last weekend and suggested to Imam Bashir Rafiq that an early visit to Birmingham may prove helpful. He has in mind the afternoon of Saturday, June 3, and may have written to you already proposing a visit that afternoon.

If you have not heard from him yet in that context and consider that date convenient you may get in touch with him yourself and settle the details with him.

Kindly convey my greetings to all our friends.

With kindest regards,

Yours sincerely,

Zafrulla Khan

M.U. Dard, Esq.,
50, The Broadway,
Perry Barr,
Birmingham B20 3EA,
England.

The minutes of the monthly meetings held on 2nd July 1972 at 31, Springfield Road, Kings Heath show Master Ahmad Krishan Dard recited the Holy Quran. Mr. Abdul Wase Adam Chughtai recited a poem of the Promised Messiah. Mr. M. U. Dard informed the community that Hudson's Book Shop had started selling Ahmadiyya books. Maulana Abdul Wahab Adam, the Deputy Imam and Mr. Bashir Ahmad Hayat visited Birmingham on Friday the 20th April, 1973. Maulana A. W. Adam led the Juma Prayers at Dr. Nazir Ahmad's house. He also addressed the community regarding the Nusrat Jahan Scheme in a special meeting. Mr. B. A. Hayat stayed a few days more in Birmingham and helped us to collect the N. J. Fund.

I wanted to do a doctorate in Theology. I proposed to do research on the Ahmadiyya Movement in Great Britain at the University of Birmingham. The University consulted my referees Sir. M. Z. Khan and Professor A. Salam about my suitability for research. My topic was approved, and I started my studies in the 1972-73 academic year. I produced a chapter on 'The Concept of Mission in Islam' in early 1974, which did not please my supervisor, who was an employee of Selly Oak Colleges, Methodist Mission. We argued about verse 105 in chapter 3 of the Holy Quran. "And let there be among you a body of men who should invite to goodness, and enjoin equity and forbid evil". My supervisor and I did not see eye to eye on the concept of mission referred to in this verse of the Holy Quran.

Ahmadies were declared non-Muslims by Zulfikar Ali Bhutto, the Prime Minister of Pakistan. My new responsibilities as the Head of Home/school Liaison Department for three schools (Nursery, Infant and Junior) resulted in the suspension of the research at my request in September 1974.

In 1973, Ahmadies were declared non-Muslim in Azad Kashmir. We were able to enlist the support of some enlightened post graduate students of the Joint Union. Guilds of students. Pakistan Society, University of Aston, Birmingham. The secretary of the Pakistani society, Mr. Muhammad Maqbool Ahmad a PhD scholar got the following resolution adopted by the society. A copy of this was sent to the Imam of the London Mosque. After completing his doctorate Dr. Muhammad Maqbool Ahmad went to Pakistan. He is now a Professor of Biological sciences at the Qaid-e-Azam University, Islamabad, Pakistan.
THE JOINT UNION
Guilds of students
University of Aston
Birmingham Polytechnic
PAKISTAN SOCIETY

As we have read in newspapers, the Azad Kashmir Government has unleashed a wave of terror and repression against students and on progressive forces in the country. The QAIYUM government is systematically building a police state under the guise of Religion and Democracy.
Pakistan Society in its Executive Committee meeting condemns the resolution adopted by the Azad Kashmir Legislative Assembly declaring Ahmadies a non-Muslim minority and banned the propagation of 'Ahmadiyyat' in the area. The Committee also condemns that the AHMEDIS be registered and should get representation in various walks of life on the basis of their being a non-Muslim minority. We call upon the people of A. K. and the people of Pakistan to expose this unrealistic, appalling and disgusting attitude of the Assembly towards Ahmadiyya Community in the area. We Know that such tactics are always used by the ruling class to divert the attention of the masses from their real cause.
We, in the interest of the people and the country ask the President of AZAD Kashmir to reconsider the resolution and withdraw it as soon as possible, because such resolutions can affect the unity among the people and can lead to the division of the country which is so vital at the moment.
Muhammad Maqbool Ahmad
SECRETARY, PAKISTAN SOCIETY
MMA/BN/15
15.5.73.

In 1974 Ahmadies were also declared non-Muslim in Pakistan. I issued a statement on the subject, which was published in the Birmingham Evening Mail.

"Birmingham Evening Mail" 10th September, 1974.
Sect warns of violence.
The head of a Muslim sect in Birmingham warned today that a move to make 10,000,000 members of the sect second-class citizens, could have repercussions in the Midlands.
Mr. Matiullah Dard, President of the city's Ahmadiyya Muslim Community, said that as part of an election move, the Pakistan leaders had declared members of the sect non-Muslims.
'We have about 200 members of the sect in Birmingham and this means they will be laughed and jeered at by other Muslims in the area" said Mr. Dard. This would result in friction and could lead to isolated incidents and violence among religious sects, he warned.
This statement was included in the book 'From the World Press - Volume 1 ", published by the Missionary in charge and Imam of the London Mosque.
Protest letters were sent to MPs in the House of Commons, London, by many members of the community. The following' telegrams were sent to Pakistan ministers:

An Ahmadiyya Muslim   40

Telegrams Sent To Pakistan On 2nd June 1974

(1) Mr. Z. A. Bhutto
Prime Minister of Pakistan, Islamabad
shocked and grieved at killing of innocent Ahmadies in Punjab.
Urge protection of Ahmadi Life and property.
Matiullah Dard,
President
Ahmadiyya Muslim Community, Birmingham

(2) The Chief Minister, Punjab, Lahore.
Shocked and grieved at killing of innocent Ahmadies in Punjab.
Urge protection of Ahmadi life and property.
Matiullah Dard
President, Ahmadiyya Community, Birmingham

(3) The Home Minister of Pakistan, Islamabad
Shocked and grieved at killing of Ahmadies in Punjab.
Urge protection of Ahmadi life and property.
Matiullah Dard
President, Ahmadiyya Community,
Birmingham

The Right Honourable John Hubert Lee, MP,
50 The Broadway
Handsworth Constituency, Perry Barr
House of Commons, Birmingham B2O 3EA
House of Parliament 26th June 1974
Westminster,
London SW1

Dear Mr. Lee,

You may have observed reports appearing in the national press about atrocities being committed against a peace-loving loyal community, the Ahmadiyya Muslims, in Pakistan. Although I am a British national, I have my relatives living in Pakistan. Acts of violence and intimidation continue. 27 Innocent Ahmadies have been killed 1,100 houses and shops have been looted and burnt. 2,000 Ahmadies made homeless. Beleaguered Ahmadies are being denied food and water or facilities to bury their dead.

Fanatical orthodox mobs have mounted an orgy of violence against the Ahmadies who are accused of heresy. Sir, you and your fellow MPs are cherished for your

An Ahmadiyya Muslim 41

recognition of human rights. The Charter of Human Rights extends to freedom of faith. I, humbly implore your intervention in this matter so that these atrocities stop forthwith and our brethren can return to normal lives.
Yours sincerely,
M. U. Dard
Member Birmingham Community Relations Committee
President Ahmadiyya Muslim Community, Birmingham

Mr. Nasir Ahmad Mubasher served the Ahmadiyya Muslim Community as a General Secretary with distinction for a year from 1974 to 1975.

FIJI HIGH COMMISSION
Our Ref: H1/10/4

25, UPPER BROOK STREET,
LONDON, W1Y 1PD.
01-493 6515

29 October, 1974.

Dear Mr. Dard,

Thank you very much for participating in our Inter Faith Service which was held in the Commonwealth Institute Theatre on Sunday, 13 October 1974. Even though the notice given was short, you willingly accepted to participate in the service and for this we are most grateful.

You will recall that in approaching you about participating in the Thanksgiving Service we had indicated that it should be in keeping with the harmonious multi-racial and multi-religious character of Fiji. The spirit in which you participated not only helped us to achieve our own aim but also made the Service the notable success that it was.

I trust that our paths will continue to cross in the future.

With warm good wishes,

Yours sincerely,

(J. R. Rabukawaqa)
High Commissioner

M. U. Dard Esq.,
50 The Broadway,
Perry Bar,
Birmingham B20 3EA.

Cession of Fiji to Great Britain Centenary Commemoration

The Fijian High Commissioner held an Inter-Faith Service to commemorate the Centenary cession of Fiji to Great Britain at the Commonwealth Institute Theatre, London, on 13th October 1974. He invited me to attend and represent Islam by reading a few relevant passages from the Holy Quran as a representative of the Muslim Community. I had met him previously at a Muslim Wedding Reception in London when he came to know about my work in Fiji in the early sixties at Lautoka Muslim High School. I consider myself very fortunate and honoured to have taken part in the Thanksgiving Service.

I have fond memories of the "Paradise of the South pacific" I had met the then governor of Fiji, Sir Kenneth Maddock at a reception given in his honour by the citizens of Nandi In 1963. He had been working in West Africa before coming to Fiji. we talked about the Ahmadiyya Muslim Community and he told me that he knew about the Ahmadiyya Movement even in Nigeria.

Ahmadiyya Contribution to The Community Health Councils

West Midlands Regional Health Authority appointed me on behalf of the Ahmadiyya Muslim Community as a member of the East Birmingham Community Health Council, a voluntary organization, from 1975 to 1983.
I persuaded the CHC to appoint Interpreters of Asian Languages for the benefit of Ethnic Minority patients in the hospitals. They were also made aware of the dietary needs of Muslin patients. Dr. M. Zakariya Tahir was appointed to the North Birmingham CHC for four years. The Birmingham Evening Mail and Community Health Council News published the following news:

EVENING MAIL-Tuesday 18th March 1975
"The Fat of Swine" Poses A Problem
The religious problem that sparked off the Indian Mutiny is causing trouble in West Midland hospitals according to a worried team of Health Service watchdogs.
They are to investigate the N.H.S. diet offered to Asians who fear that they might taste "the fat of swine" - strictly prohibited for orthodox Muslims.
East Birmingham Community Health Council was told by a coloured member Mr. M. U. Dard, that Muslims would prefer packed lunches, prepared if necessary outside hospitals, rather than risk offending their religious scruples.

Mr. J. H, Hoare, District Nursing Officer, said that at one time an attempt was made to supply a printed menu. But the idea was abandoned when it was found that the patients concerned could not read it. And a Hindu cook might not be satisfactory to a Muslim even if one were employed. Mr. D. Whipp said if cooks of various religion were employed to prepare special diets he was not surprised that Muslims and Hindus were rejecting food.
The council decided to appoint Mr. Dard to make a special investigation.

EVENING MAIL-Wednesday 14th January, 1976
Hospital plan to get interpreter, A Birmingham hospital plan to solve patients language problems by taking on an interpreter.
The main difficulties are said to be with Asians who cannot describe their illnesses or symptoms because they do not speak English.
Some of them are known to have stopped attending hospitals because of language barrier, East Birmingham
Community Health Council was told:

An Ahmadiyya Muslim

But now East Birmingham Hospital is to employ a full-time interpreter to help patients, nurses and doctors.

Mr. M. U. Dard a member of the health council said: "I understand the hospital is to advertise the post next month.

"There is a definite need for the service and it should be met adequately if the right candidate can be found."

EVENING MAIL - Wednesday 4th August, 1976 Hospital Religion Move A Chaplain specialising in eastern religions may be appointed to help immigrant patients at East Birmingham hospital.

Hospital Administrator Mr. John Yates told East Birmingham Community Health Council that a survey would be carried out to find out how many Hindus, Muslims or Sikhs wanted the service.

Mr. M. U. Dard who represents the Ahmadiyya Muslim Community on the council had said there are six Christian ministers holding part-time appointments at the hospital.

Three are Church of England, one is Catholic and two are Free Church. Ministers from several faiths can visit patients but appointed chaplains have greater access to the hospital facilities.

They work on a Rota, receive weekly payment and hold regular services for staff and patients.

CHC NEWS- October 1978 CHC television contract with Asians
Geoffrey Johnson, Secretary, East Birmingham CHC
East Birmingham. CHC has recently had the chance to contribute to a nation-wide Asian TV programme and it seems likely that our representative will soon be invited to make a number of further appearances to enlarge on the work of CHCs.

One of the main problems faced by CHCs in the West Midlands and mostly by most other CHCs representing a sizable number of Asian NHS users, has been the diffidence of Asian patients in raising health care problems, either with CHCs or other bodies. Those CHCs which have tried to make contact with Asian minorities in their districts will appreciate the value of this new opportunity for contact and the importance of maintaining the quality of our input.

We would therefore like to hear from CHCs in other regions who has been involved with Asian patients and their families. The CHCs spokesperson on this programme is Mr. M. U. Dard an Asian with a full command of all the major Indian dialects, and a founder member of the CHC. Mr. Dard may be contacted direct at his home, 50 The Broadway, Birmingham. B20 3EA (021-356-7648) or through the CHC office at 203 Bordesley Green East, Birmingham B9 5SP (021 784 5388).

203 Bordesley Green East
Birmingham B9 5SP
Telephone: 021-7845388

Mr. M U Dard
4 Goffs Close
Harborne Rise, California Way
Birmingham 32

Dear Mr. Dard,

I am writing to express my own and the CHC's thanks for all your hard work over many years on the CHC's behalf It is unfortunate that your organisation was not successful in the recent elections. as we can ill afford to lose such experienced members as yourself. Please accept my best wishes for the future.

Yours sincerely,

Betty E Wilson
Chairman 28th August, 1984
East Birmingham Community Health Council
Chairman: Miss B E Wilson
Secretary: Paul Rooney

The Ahmadiyya Muslim Community took part in all good causes to promote harmony and peace. Allah had blessed the community in everything, and within a few years the name of the Ahmadiyya Muslim Association became well respected, particularly among the educated sections of the City of Birmingham.

The Fourth Nasir Tarbiyyati class was organized by the Ahmadiyya Muslim Mission, U. K. at Mahmud Hall, London from 24th, December 1982 to 1st, January 1983 under the supervision of Maulana Sheikh Murbarak Ahmad Amir and Missionary in charge. The syllabus included the Holy Quran, The Hadith, The History of Islam, Islamic Teachings, Distinctive Features of Ahmadiyyat comparative studies and practical teaching. Three Lecturers from Birmingham taught.

Many Ahmadiyya children from all over the U. K. attended the course 105 students from 22 cities participated, and Dr. Prof. Salam, the Nobel Laureate in Physics addressed the student in one of the sessions. The Ahmadiyya bulletin dated February 1982 published a full report with photographs.

An Ahmadiyya Muslim

Matiullah Dard with his son Dr. Ahmed Krishan Dard

My son Ahmad Krishan Dard obtained his first degree of Bachelor of Science from the University of London in 1983. My father passed away in the same year at Rabwah. He was born on the 16th of May 1908, ten days before the demise of the Promised Messiah on the 26th May 1908. My father died on the 3rd of July 1983, at the age of 75 years. Hadhrat Mirza Tahir Ahmad Khalifatul Masih IV led his funeral prayer. My father was a "Moosi". so he was buried in the Bahishti Maqbarah, Rabwah, Pakistan. May Allah grant him a lofty place in Paradise. Amin.

In 1975, Chaudhary Abdul Hafeez was elected as the President of the community. I was elected to serve as Financial and Preaching secretary.
Sometime later in 1986, Mirza Muhammad Siddique was appointed as Financial Secretary, and I continued as Preaching Secretary. I was invited to give lectures on the various aspects of Islam on many occasions at different Institutions of Learning in the West Midlands. I was requested by the college of St Paul and St Mary Cheltenham Teacher Training College to give a lecture on the teachings of Islam during which time I not only talked about women in Islam but also distributed the famous book "The Philosophy of the teachings of Islam" by Hadhrat Mirza Ghulam Ahmad.

Mirza Naseer Ahmad the Regional Missionary and I visited schools, colleges, universities, peace fairs and many houses to distribute Islamic literature and to explain the beauties of Islam.

The National Schools Committee

In 1983 I was invited to join The National Schools Committee. The committee was setup with two aims. These were to investigate the feasibility of establishing an Ahmadiyya school but with a multi-faith foundation; each child would receive a high standard of Infant and Junior education but each child would be Taught Religious Education by a teacher of their own faith. The school would be Grant Maintained. The second aim of The Committee was to write the Religious Syllabus based upon the lives of prophets and basic principles and moral teachings of individual faiths. What we hoped to achieve was in direct contrast to the Muslim schools that were beginning to emerge. The Committee met six times in late 1983, but attendance and progress were slow. The founder members were Mr. Nasir Ward who was Chairman, Mr. Rashid Ahmed, Secretary, Mr. Muhammad Ahmad, President of Croydon, Mr. Ismail B. K. Addo of Peckham and myself from Birmingham. There were other contributors who helped us greatly but there were others who although members and for reasons best known to themselves, neither attended nor made a positive contribution.

Under the guidance of the then Amir, Maulana Ataul Mujeeb Rashed the Committee was expanded to include Mirza Naseer Ahmad, Regional Missionary for the Midlands and Mr. Michael Clarke from Birmingham. Work on producing written material was started straight away. Over the next few months I was given the task of writing a biography of the Holy Prophet Muhammad. May Allah's peace and blessings be upon him. The Life of The Promised Messiah a.s, with illustration and the story of Hadhrat Moses a.s and Pharaoh.

In January 1984 an article appeared in the 'Telegraph and Argus' a local newspaper describing our proposal to take over a soon to be redundant school in Kirklees. There was an extreme reaction by some anti-Ahmadiyya Mullahs who put pressure on the Kirklees Council. The Chairman and Secretary and some other members of the National Schools Committee went to Kirklees to put our case to the council. They were sympathetic but non-committal. The work continued in a very friendly and productive manner and we completed several final drafts with illustrations which were designed and drawn mainly by Mrs. Qudsiyya Ward and Miss Nasira Noor.

March 30th 1984 saw the arrival in London of our beloved Khalifa, Hadhrat Mirza Tahir Ahmad and we continued our work under his instructions. A young Einglishman named Tahir Selby joined our Committee. He had dedicated his life to becoming an Ahmadiyya Missionary which required him to go to Rabwah. His leaving party held on September 8th 1984, was intended to be informal but so many people wanted to pay their heartfelt respects to him that it turned into a formal occasion with farewell speeches given by the Imam Maulana Ataul Mujeeb Rashed, The General Secretary Chaudhary Hadayat Ullah Bangvi and Mr. Ismail B. K. Addo among others.

The Committee met throughout 1984 in London, Croydon and Birmingham and I have fond memories of the kindness shown to us by members of those Jama'ats in providing us with delicious meals and accommodation.

Towards the end of 1984 Huzoor instructed The Committee that it would be more appropriate to find a suitable location within easy reach of London which could be used for large gatherings, accommodation and for training and education. Our application to Kirklees council was withdrawn and the Chairman and secretary assisted the National Executive in looking for suitable sites. One of those turned out to be the old Sheep hatch school near Tilford in surrey which became Islamabad.

The work of the Committee ended when we handed over our completed work to Imam Sahib who would arrange for it to be reviewed and published.

Master Hari Parasad & Matiullah Dard invigilating an exam at Lautoka Muslim High School 1962

Zia's Persecution of Ahmadies

General Zia, President of Pakistan, promulgated decrees against Ahmadiyya Muslims, and started persecuting them. I issued the following statements in the Birmingham Evening Mail, the Birmingham Post and the Daily News during 1984 and 1985: Birmingham.

EVENING MAIL- Tuesday May 1st, 1984
Followers of separatist Muslim faith in Birmingham say they are terrified for the safety of their families in Pakistan after a new ordinance banning their religion. Believers of the Ahmadiyya Muslim teachings left in Pakistan face public ridicule and even imprisonment if they continue to worship the traditional ways, the country's president General Zia has announced. They have been ordered not to pray to God, not refer to their place of worship as a mosque and not to use Islamic terms, with a penalty of three years imprisonment say local leaders. And even in England Ahmadiyya Muslims face jeering and taunts from the rest of the Muslim Community. Mr. Matiullah Dard, the preaching secretary of the Ahmadiyya Muslim community in Birmingham said: "We are being prevented from practicing our religion. This is a very retrograde step and is attacking the basic principles on which Pakistan is founded"

**Mr & Mrs Abdul Latif with Matiullah Dard
at the Nandi International Airport, Fiji 1962**

> ## The Birmingham Post
> No. 38,946 18p Wednesday, May 30, 1984 Midland Edition
>
> Mr Matiullah Dard, preaching secretary of the 500-strong Ahmadi movement in the West Midlands, who says the sect is being persecuted in Pakistan.
>
> ## Sect fears persecution
>
> You walk through a bauble factory, past a butcher-shop and there, in a deserted cemetery in Srinagar, capital of Kashmir, you see the tomb of Jesus Christ under a corrugated roof.
>
> According to the 11 million adherents of a Muslim sect based in Pakistan, Jesus was physically revived after His crucifixion and later travelled to Kashmir where he lived and preached for another 30 years.
>
> That is an article of faith for the Ahmadis and they preach it vigorously throughout the world — including Birmingham — and in their headquarters at the town of Rabwah, on the Chenab River in Pakistani Kashmir.
>
> ### Quirk
>
> Mainstream Muslims have no objection to this, feeling it just another odd little quirk of the Ahmadis.
>
> Where the mainstream Orthodox Muslims fall out with the Ahmadis is over the latter's claim that their leader Hazrat Mirza Ahmad, born in 1855, was a prophet chosen by Allah. Orthodox thought is that Mohammed was the last prophet, which makes the Ahmadis heretical.
>
> The Ahmadis, who insist they have an unmatched record in Pakistan for their success in trade and industry and have achieved a 100 per cent literacy rate in Rabwah, say they are used as pawns whenever the Pakistani government feels it needs to underline its own orthodoxy.
>
> "Now persecution of the Ahmadis has started again in Pakistan, the country we helped to found," says Mr. Matiullah Dard, the Preaching Secretary of the 500-strong Ahmadi movement in the West Midlands.
>
> "We are hearing daily from our families in Pakistan that at least five of our faith have lost their lives at the hands of Muslim zealots.
>
> "Yet when Jinnah founded Pakistan, it was with the urging of my uncle, Imam Abdul Rahim Dard, who persuaded him to return to Pakistan to take over the leadership of the Muslim League.
>
> "The Imam was head of the Ahmadi mosque in Putney — the first mosque in Britain — and Jinnah later wrote that 'The persuasive eloquence of the Imam left me no escape'."
>
> Mr Dard, who teaches Urdu to Muslim children at Birmingham schools, sees the danger of anti-Ahmadi feeling both as Muslim and as a Pakistani.
>
> "With a stroke of his pen, General Zia has made us all second-rate citizens," he says. "We are thus open to exploitation by all Orthodox Muslims. Imagine this happening to Methodists or Baptists in the UK.
>
> "If the Ahmadis, a small minority in Pakistan, seek to defend themselves, the Russians will have just the same excuse to walk into Pakistan as they used when they walked into Afghanistan — as alleged peace-keepers."
>
> From the Pakistan Embassy in London, Mr. Qutubuddin Aziz, Chief Information Officer, said he had heard nothing of Ahmadis being killed in Pakistan.
>
> ### Ignored
>
> "But the sect was declared unMuslim in 1974 under Mr. Bhutto, when they refused to acknowledge that Mohammed was the last Prophet. They ignored orders that they could not carry out any activities in the name of Islam so, last month, General Zia again clamped down on them.
>
> "They are no longer allowed to call their places of worship mosques — mosques are used only by Muslims, nor are they permitted to make the Azan, their call to prayer, in public. They can hold religious services, but they must not describe them as Muslim services. "It may seem harsh but it is the Muslim way. We believe that Mohammed was the last Prophet and that is that."
>
> **MAUREEN MESSENT**

You walk through a bauble factory, past a butcher shop and there in a deserted cemetery in Srinagar, capital of Kashmir, you see the tomb of Jesus Christ under a corrugated roof. According to the 11 million adherents of a Muslim sect based in Pakistan, Jesus was physically revived after His crucifixion and later travelled to Kashmir where he lived and preached for another 80 years.

That is an article of faith for the Ahmadis and they preach it vigorously throughout the world - including Birmingham and in their headquarters at the town of Rabwah, on the Chenab River in Pakistani Kashmir.

An Ahmadiyya Muslim   51

Quirk

Mainstream Muslims have no objection to this, feeling it just another odd little quirk of the Ahmadis.

Where the mainstream orthodox Muslim fall out with the Ahmadis is over the latter's claim that their leader Hadhrat Mirza Ahmad, born in 1835 was a Prophet chosen by Allah. Orthodox thought is that Mohammed was the last Prophet, which makes the Ahmadis heretical.

The Ahmadis who insist they have an unmatched record in Pakistan for their success in trade and industry and have achieved a 100 per cent literacy rate in Rabwah, say they are used as pawns whenever the Pakistani government feels it needs to underline its own orthodoxy.

"Now persecution of the Ahmadis has started again in Pakistan, the country we helped to found," says Mr Matiullah Dard, the Preaching Secretary of the 500 strong Ahmadi in the West Midlands. "We are hearing daily from our families in Pakistan that at least five of our faith have lost their lives at the hands of Muslim zealots.
"Yet when Jinnah founded Pakistan, it was with the urging of my uncle, Imam Abdul Rahim Dard, who persuaded him to take over the leadership of the Muslim League.
"The Imam was head of the Ahmadi mosque in Putney - the first mosque in Britain - and Jinnah later wrote that "The persuasive eloquence of the Imam left me no escape."
Mr. Dard who teaches Urdu to Muslim children at Birmingham schools, sees the danger of anti-Ahmadi feeling both as Muslim and as a Pakistani.
"With a stroke of his pen, General Zia has made us all second-rate citizens." he says. "We are thus open to exploitation by all Orthodox Muslims. Imagine this happening to Methodists or Baptists in the U.K.
"If the Ahmadies, a small minority in Pakistan, seek to defend themselves, the Russians will have just the same excuse to walk into Pakistan as they used when they walked into Afghanistan - as alleged peace-keepers."
From the Pakistan Embassy in London, Mr. Qutubuddin Aziz, Chief Information Officer, said he had heard nothing of Ahmadies being killed in Pakistan.

Ignored

"But the sect was declared non Muslim in 1974 under Mr. Bhutto when they refused to acknowledged that Mohammad was the last Prophet. They ignored orders that they could not carry out any activities in the name of Islam so, last month General Zia again clamped down on them.
"They are no longer allowed to call their places of worship mosques - mosques

are used only by Muslims, nor are they permitted to make the Azan, their call to prayer, in public. They can hold religious services, but they must not describe them as Muslim services. "It may seem harsh but it is the Muslim way. We believe that Mohammed was the last Prophet and that is that."
Maureen Messent

DAILY NEWS Wednesday February 20 1985
City's Asian families fear

Birmingham Asians belonging to a religious sect fear for the safety of relatives in Pakistan.

Five members of the Ahmadiyya Muslims have already been executed for their beliefs and thousands thrown into jail.

Now Birmingham's 600 followers of the faith are stepping up their protest against "inhuman treatment" meted out to their brethren.

They are writing to MPs and the British Consulate protesting that the Pakistani government is taking away their basic human rights in barring them from practising their religion.

Matiullah Dard, Chairman of the Preaching Committee of Birmingham's Ahmadiyya movement said families in the city were very worried about the present situation.

THE BIRMINGHAM POST - Monday March 11 1985
Military war of words

Pakistan's military regime has stepped up persecution of the Ahmadi sect according to a spokesman in Birmingham. Dozens of the four million-strong community have been imprisoned for practicing their faith, claims Mr. Matiullah Dard.

Ahmadies are barred from universities and are denied promotion in the civil service and armed services, he says.

The Government discourages people from shopping at Ahmadia owned stores, attacks the movement through the controlled Press, confiscates its publications and harasses its officials, he says.

At least five Ahmadies have been murdered by Moslems zealots, Mr. Dard claims. The sect - which believes that Jesus Christ was revived after His crucifixion and later travelled to Kashmir, where he preached for another 80 years - has 11 million adherents world-wide, 500 in the West Midlands.

Their success - one won the Nobel Prize for Physics six years ago - has earned them the nickname "The Jews of Islam." Their problems began in 1974 when President Bhutto declared that the sect was not Moslem.

The Ahmadies claim that their founder, Hadhrat Mirza Ahmed, who was born in 1835, was a prophet chosen by Allah. This outrages many orthodox Muslims who told that Mohammed was the last prophet.

Regime

Last year, general Zia's Islamic fundamentalist regime - claiming that the Ahmadies have ignored orders to cease carrying out activities in the name of Islam - banned them from describing their places of worship as mosques. According to Mr. Dard who teaches Urdu at Birmingham schools, the authorities are now imprisoning Ahmadis who refuse to stop displaying Islam's most sacred text, the Kalima, which states "There is no god but God and Mohammed is His prophet." The Pakistan Embassy in London denies the allegations. A spokesman said "There was a report last autumn that a person died in a family feud and he was said to be an Ahmadi."
To provoke Moslems and the authorities, some Ahmadis at one or two places in Punjab painted the Kalima on their places of worship, trying to give the impression these were Islamic mosques. This was resented and the authorities ordered them not to do so lest it create communal trouble. A couple of arrests were made."
Ahmadis continue to serve in the Forces and civil service, some in senior positions. At Rabwah the police give Ahmadis protection under law.
"There is no Government Press. Some private papers at times criticise the Ahmadis, just as the Ahmadis make propaganda against Moslems and the Government in their publications."
Thomas Quirke

DAILY NEWS Wednesday March 20,1985
Newsletters

Unfair to Islam

SIR - I was alarmed to read the letter Islam by M. Hussain of Sparkbrook.
In order to become a Muslim one does not need any certificate from the Pakistan government or the so called Muslims living in this country. According to the prophet Mohammad only Allah knows the reality. It is up to each and every human being to declare what he believes in and what they do not believe in.
The Holy Quran says there is no compulsion in religion. If Allah had decreed it, he would have made everyone a Muslim, but he did not.
Why is M. Hussain acting against the teachings of Quran and forcing his brand on the Ahmadiyya Muslims? As far as the persecution of Ahmadiyya Muslims is concerned, I can provide documentary evidence of the Inhuman treatment by the Pakistan Government and Mullahs. They have so far put 80 people behind bars merely because they have inscribed the Kalima on their clothes and in the form of badges and stickers on their cars.
The so called Muslims like M. Hussain of Sparkbrook are out to destroys this Kalima.
Kamran Chughtai, Kings Heath

DAILY NEWS Tuesday April 23 1985
Newsletters

Muslims

SIR - A few letters have been published for and against the Ahmadiyya Muslims. The letters of M. Clarke and K. Chughtai were sensible I am amazed to read another letter by M. Hussain in which he exposes himself as in ignorant man, self conceited and absolutely devoid of reason - like the fanatic Mullahs.
The following Quranic description is fitting: "Their case is like the case of a person who kindled a fire and when it lighted up all around him, Allah took away their light and left them in thick darkness, they see not, they are deaf, dumb and blind so they will not return."

Prophet Mohammed had already decided the issue of calling a Muslim a disbeliever. "Abu Dharr relates that he heard the Holy Prophet say: If one of you should call another a disbeliever or enemy of Allah and he should in fact not be such, the title will revert to the one who uttered it."
- A. Krishan, Washwood Heath.

Chairman Preaching Committee

In July 1984, I was appointed as Chairman of the Preaching Committee.
We organised public meetings, book stalls and held preaching days regularly. We celebrated the Religious Founders day, in which representatives of other religions spoke about their respective founders.

These multi cultural and multi-religious meetings were greatly appreciated by all concerned. They helped to create an atmosphere of peace and co-operation among peoples in the cosmopolitan City of Birmingham.

The London Mosque

16 GRESSENHALL ROAD, LONDON SW18 5QL. TEL: 01-874 6298 CABLES: ISLAMABAD LONDON
01-874 7590
TELEX: 28604 MON REF. G1292

REF............................ DATE... 11/6/84

بِسْمِ اللهِ الرَّحْمٰنِ الرَّحِيْمِ

عزیزم مکرم مطیع اللہ درد!
السلام علیکم ورحمۃ اللہ وبرکاتہ

آپ کا خط ملا۔ آپ کی تجویز اور مشورہ بہت اچھا ہے۔ آپ کو اجازت ہے۔ جزاکم اللہ تعالیٰ۔ اللہ تعالیٰ آپ کے ساتھ ہو اور اس دعاؤں کو قبول کرے اور اہل احمدیت کی خاطر قبولیت دعا کے جلسے برپا اور جمع پر دل نظارے رکھے۔

والسلام
خاکسار
مرزا طاہر احمد
خلیفۃ المسیح الرابع

[additional handwritten note follows]

P.T.O.

An Ahmadiyya Muslim   56

Rev. Billy Graham Challenged

In June 1984, I requested Hadhrat Mirza Tahir Ahmad Khalifatul Masih IV to allow me to challenge Dr. Billy Graham, the visiting Evangelist of America, who was proclaiming the Christian Gospel during this year through "Mission England", to a prayer duel as prescribed by the Promised Messiah, for the recovery of clinically despaired patients. Hadhrat Mirza Tahir Ahmad Khalifatul Masih kindly gave me permission as a Preaching Secretary of the Ahmadiyya Muslim Community Birmingham to invite Dr. Billy Graham to the challenge originally issued by the Promised Messiah Hadhrat Mirza Ghulam Ahmad. and so, with the blessings of my beloved Khalifa, I sent the following letter to Dr. Billy Graham.

To: Rev. Billy Graham　　　　　　　　Ahmadiyya Muslim Mission
The Visiting Evangelist　　　　　　　792 Washwood Heath Road,
In Birmingham　　　　　　　　　　　Birmingham B8 2JL

19th June, 1984

Dear Sir,
In our time relations between religions seem to change from phase to phase. Hostile at one time, they have tended to become tolerant, perhaps even sympathetic and friendly. It is time they also became fruitful in terms of the discovery of truth. They have not been fruitful because parties to religious controversies have set no rules, prescribed no limits or controls over their advocacy. Each exchange seems like a race run without rules.
If statements on behalf of a book and arguments in support of those statements are taken and based on the book, parties to a discussion of the merits of holy books would assess the merits of those books instead of assessing the merits of their exponents.
To promote a universal outlook in matters spiritual we have to put some kind of order in our discussion of religion.
Today religion is fighting a rearguard action. It is being assailed from every direction and appears sore pressed.
The central and most vital value in religion is faith in a Supreme Creator. Even this citadel of faith is now under assault. One hears pronouncements like; God is dead or God is only the centre of our being or we should drop the very word God from our vocabulary.
The truth, nevertheless, is and this is fundamental to all faiths that God is as Supreme today as He was before. He created the world and man. All His

attributes continue in operation all the time. For instance He hears prayer and communicates with His righteous servants as He was wont to do in ages past. It is open to any one of us to establish, maintain and strengthen communion with our Maker by following the guidance revealed by Him.

We have the fullest assurance today, for instance, that God hears and answers the prayer of His righteous servants.

The only method of restoring faith in the existence and Majesty of the Supreme Creator is the witnessing of His Living signs. This can, for instance be done through prayer and manifestation of God's attribute of the Acceptor of prayer.

The Founder of the Ahmadiyya Movement, Ahmad of Qadian (1835-1908) called the followers of all faiths to establish the truth of their respective faiths through a sign of the acceptance of prayer, but none of them was willing to respond to his call in the capacity of a representative of his faith.

His fourth successor, the present head of the Ahmadiyya Movement, Hadhrat Mirza Tahir Ahmad has renewed this call. And I as the Preaching Secretary of the Ahmadiyya movement in Birmingham address the following communication to you Rev. Billy Graham. The communication is self explanatory.

" I have to give you the glad tidings that he for whom the Christians and the Muslims have been waiting, has appeared and had illumined the world with his light and filled it with his glory.

Nation had risen against nation and famines, wars, earthquakes, pestilences and iniquity abound, and the sun and the moon have darkened and the stars have fallen from heaven and the power of heaven have been shaken and the sign of the Son of Man has appeared in heaven. So, as the lightening cometh out of the East, and shineth even unto the West, the coming of the Son of Man has been.

He appeared in India, which is the east, and which has been from ancient days the seat of knowledge and learning and very soon his teachings were propagated in the farthest corners of the earth, so that his followers are to be found in all continents of Asia. Africa, Europe and America.

The Prophet Ahmad of Qadian (1835-1908) appeared in India, in the power and spirit of Christ as John the Baptist came in the power and spirit of Elias, and everything was written in the scriptures with regard to his coming has been fulfilled, even the gathering of the Jews in Palestine.

To convince you of the truth and righteousness of Ahmad of Qadian I one of the least and humblest of his followers and servant venture to propose a decisive test for your most serious consideration and acceptance. Jesus Christ said, " A good tree bringeth not forth corrupt fruit; neither a corrupt tree bring forth good fruit. For every tree is known by its fruits". Again he has said, "Verily I say unto you, if you have faith as a grain of mustard seed, ye shall say unto this mountain, remove hence to yonder place; and it shall remove, and nothing shall be impossible to you." Again he has said, " And all things whatsoever ye shall ask in prayer, believing, ye shall receive." A living faith, must exhibit the signs of life, and we the followers of Hadhrat Ahmad realize within ourselves that Islam, our faith, is a living faith. We firmly believe that should you as the Well Known Evangelist, be prepared to put to the test the truth of Islam and Christianity, God will surely cause the good tree to bring forth good fruit and He shall not give His beloved son a serpent for a fish or a stone for bread, but shall open for him and shall accept his prayers.

We have time after time invited Christian divines to have recourse to this test, but none has so far ventured to come forward. I approach you therefore, and through your Evangelical crusade every other Christian divine in the world, with the request that we may all pray for the achievement of a certain difficult object, in order to demonstrate the truth of our respective faiths. For instance, let us take a certain number of sick persons whose life is clinically despaired of and then divide them among ourselves by lot and let the Christian church pray for the recovery of those allotted to it and we shall pray for the recovery of those allotted to us and let the world witness the sign of God's grace and mercy being vouchsafed in answer to the humble supplications of those of His servants who adhere firmly to the truth. In accordance with the test laid down by Jesus Christ, the prayers of His believing righteous servants will find gracious acceptance with God and the majority of those allotted to them will recover, while the maladies of the majority of those allotted to me, other party, will follow their normal course in accordance with medical opinion.

In conclusion, I entreat you to ponder over this humble offer in all sincerity, as I have conveyed to you these tidings of the kingdom of Heaven out of the fullness of my love, for in the presence of God we are all equal."

Yours sincerely

Matiullah Dard
Preaching secretary
Ahmadiyya Movement in Islam
Birmingham

BBC Radio News

The following news was broadcast on 25.6. 1984 at 6.30 am and 7.00 am in the News Bulletin on the West Midland Radio of the BBC, Birmingham.
"A Birmingham Muslim Leader has challenged American Evangelist Billy Graham to a miracle match during his visit to the city next week. The Preaching secretary of the 500 strong Ahmadiyya Islamic Movement, Matiullah Dard, thinks that the prayer duel will show that the Muslim beliefs are more authentic than Christian beliefs. He says he and Dr. Graham should perform their miracles on a group of sick people. 'We could do them a service and draw lots - Billy Graham and his people can have half of them and we can have half of them and they could pray in their churches according to their religion and we will pray in our mosques according to the religion of Islam. And we believe that God will, most certainly, show this sign of the Prayer and the patients who would have been allotted to us would most certainly, recover. That would certainly show that the God definitely listens to the Prayers of the Ahmadiyya Muslims".

Mr. John Taynton of the Commercial Radio BRMB invited me for an interview about the challenge. The radio interview lasted for ten minutes and is preserved on an audiocassette.

Transcript of the interview broadcast on The 25th June 1984

" Well Billy Graham's visit has already caused quite a minor storm in religious circles. Mr. Matiullah Dard who's the chairman of the preaching committee of the Ahmadiyya moment in Islam in Birmingham, has issued a challenge to Dr. Graham to a religious debate. Mr. Dard says Billy Graham should acknowledge that Christianity as an independent religion does not exist and what he should be converting people to is Islam. Now that's fairly controversial point of view from a group which although it was the first Islamic group in Britain to build a Mosque is considered to be non Moslem by other Islamic groups in Pakistan for instance which is a strict Moslem country.
You can be jailed if you are a follower of the Ahmadiyya movement and call yourself Moslem. Well to tell us why he has issued a challenge to Billy Graham, Matiullah Dard is with us in the studio." Thank you very much for coming in"
'Well let's ask you that question directly. Why have you challenged Billy Graham?" "Well the founder of the Ahmadiyya movement Ahmad of Qadian called the follower of all faiths to establish the truth of their respective faiths

through a sign of the acceptance of prayer but not one of them was willing to respond to this call in the capacity of a representative of his faith. His fourth successor the present head of the Ahmadiyya movement Hadhrat Mirza Tahir Ahmad has renewed his call and I as the preaching secretary and the chairman of the preaching committee has issued this challenge to Dr. Billy Graham. ''

" Well what exactly do you want him to do then. Explain to us exactly what you're after?"

" For instance. Let us take a certain number of sick persons, who's life is clinically despaired of and then divide them among ourselves by lot and let the Christian Church pray for the recovery of those allotted to it and we shall pray for the recovery of those allotted to us and let the world witness the sign of God's grace and mercy being vouchsafed in answer to the humble supplications."

" What your are saying is that you want a sort of prayer challenge, to see which group the most power?"

"No. The idea is that if we claim that God loves us and our religion is the living religion then we should show some sign to prove that God really listens to our prayers and answers back to us. For instance the non Ahmadiyya people claim that God does not speak nowadays but we claim that He speaks as He used to speak in the past and answers all the prayers and we have got thousands of examples in the Ahmadiyya movement."

"But isn't it rather asking a lot to expect any religious person to - to submit to a, to a challenge of curing people by prayer, surely no religious organisation would want to take up a challenge like that?"

" But this challenge is not thrown to Tom, Dick and Harry really. it is a challenge between the representatives of religions otherwise, it will become a mockery and it is a very serious matter, and the founder of our movement has given it a great deal of thought and decided that we should show this sign between the religious leaders and representatives so that the truth can be ascertained and we are sure that most certainly we can show that living God's connection with the Ahmadiyya movement in Islam which is really the true Islamic theology represented today."

" Well, I'll come to that point in a moment. But isn't really a greater way to understanding between religions is to sit down and talk and find common ground rather than to stage what really sounds like a bit of a publicity stunt - to try to , to challenge Billy Graham on a visit to the Midlands."

" Well for that matter I would like to say to you I will quote from my challenge that in our times relations between religions seems to change from phase to phase. Hostile at one time they have tended lately to become tolerant perhaps even sympathetic and friendly. It is time they also became fruitful in terms of the discovery of the truth.

They have not been fruitful because parties to the religious controversies have set no rules, prescribed no limits or controls over their advocacy. Each exchange seems like a race run without rules. If statements on behalf of a book and arguments in support of those statements are taken from, and based on the book, parties to a discussion of the merits of the Holy books or religions would assess the merits of those religions instead of assessing the merits of...."

"With, with all due respect what your saying is, is will lose people they won't understand that at all. All they understand is Billy Graham is coming here, people who want to hear him will go to hear him people who follow your Islamic teachings will follow that. What is the purpose of trying to- to, to stage something like this, which I am sure Billy Graham will ignore."

" Well, well the purpose is to show that Christianity today is simply a part of Islam because the Holy Quran contains chapters about Jesus Christ and if I could give an analogy, that Islam is the youngest religion in the world and all the previous religions and their theology is incorporated. What I think Islam is, is the culmination of all the religions of the past which began with prophet Adam and they went through an evolution which really culminated and was made perfect by Prophet Muhammad. May Allah's peace and blessings be upon him."

" But isn't that a bit of bold statement to make for a group which isn't even recognized as truly Islamic by other Islamic groups. "

" I. I. I wouldn't think so-that the Ahmadiyya movement is nearly now eleven million all around the world and we are the most evangelical movement within Islam - we are the pioneers in many fields, in building schools, mosques translating the Holy Quran into various languages, and the other Muslims like the early Christians who persecuted by the Jews, such is the case with us we liken ourselves with Jesus Christ and his followers in the early days of Christianity and our Prophet has claimed himself as the representative of Jesus Christ in fact in one of the Islamic books the coming Messiah is mentioned as a Jesus Christ and that is a figurative name not a literal name."

"I mean its just so our listeners understand a little more about, erm your own particular group, erm as I understand it the Ahmadiyya movement in fact claims, that which is centred on Pakistan I think That's where the ...... "

"Well at the moment our headquarters are in Pakistan and we are the people who helped to build that country as well"

"But you do claim that as part of your teachings that you actually have the body of Jesus Christ buried in Kashmir."

"Well that is the arc, the historical evidence is there in fact recently a German team has gone to Srinagar Kashmir to investigate this matter, and Jesus Christ's interview has been recorded in the book which is called Bhavesh Puran with the king of Kashmir, who's name is Shalbahan, in which he has said that he was born without father and came from far away country and told him all the teachings and if you study history and anthropology you will see the Afghani people and the Kashmiri people belong to Israelite race, and in fact when Jesus came in Palestine they were only two tribes living there, other ten were made captive by the Persian king and scattered all over the middle eastern countries up to Tibet, Kashmir and Punjab and surprisingly enough Pandit Jawaher Lal Nehru wrote a book 'Glimpses from the World History', I think is the name, he also mentions the coming of Jesus and the travelling of Jesus Christ in Kashmir and Punjab."

"Now, you have sent this challenge to Dr. Billy Graham."

An Ahmadiyya Muslim 62

"I have, by the registered post and as you can see with your own eyes the acknowledgment I have received."
"Yes I have a photocopy here."
".. by somebody on his behalf has signed"
"Do you for one moment think he will accept this Challenge."
"I most sincerely hope that he does because the world needs a sign today, and we most certainly want to bring Humanity back to one God and worship of One God."
"I think if we look at the record of the Ahmadiyya movement, Billy Graham has come up today but before Billy Graham, during prophet Ahmed's life before there was another Evangelist in America called John Alexander Dowie who claimed himself as great Billy Graham and even more than him, he in fact entered into that challenge and accepted the challenge in a way and was destroyed by God Almighty."
"With all due respect I must put to you the point as a group you have I think you have 20,000 followers in this country is that right."
"Oh yeah, up to 20,000 scattered all over this country, yes"
"And Billy Graham is likely to have ten times that figure coming to see him in the Midlands."
"I think if you are judging something on merits then you do not judge it by numbers."
"But you want to judge it by numbers on which group will cure the most people that's the challenge you put to him"
"That is a test for a prescribed thing and it is one of the tests which I have proposed. If Billy Graham and his people would like to propose another one in which we could test the veracity of a religion then I am open to that."
"But you don't think support for a religion, numbers of people supporting is a test in itself."
"Well nowadays when..."
"Would you for one moment think that you could fill Villa Park 8 times over."
"Well, I'm sure that when the Ahmadiyya movements spreads that we will be able to fill more than Villa Park not one, thousands of them"
"And how long will that take do you think."
"Well our Prophet has predicted that as it took Jesus Christ three hundred years to come up on the international scene, so is the Ahmadiyya movement going to take nearly three hundred years and we feel that it will be much before that because we feel that we are the followers of Prophet Muhammad May Allah's Peace and Blessings be Upon him, who was the greatest of the Prophets."
"Will you actually be going to see Dr. Billy Graham while he is here?"
"I will wait for his response first."
"Mr. Dard thank you very much for coming in."
"It has been my pleasure talking to you. Thank you very much."

Reverend Billy Graham's Reply to the Challenge

MLR/ZT
3rd July 1984
Mr. Matiullah Dard
Preaching Secretary
Ahmadiyya Muslim Mission
792 Washwood Health Road
Birmingham
B8 2NP

Dear Mr. Dard,

I had delayed answering your letter until we had adequate time to consider our reply to you. I would not in any way want to minimize the power of prayer for physical healing, but that is not the essence of the ministry of the mission in which Mr. Graham is currently involved.

During the period of Mission England, his total energy is concentrated on the proclamation of the Christian Gospel in all its simplicity and it would not be appropriate for him to be diverted into other Christian ministry at the present time. It has been our experience over many years that those who find Christ often experience the healing power of the Holy Spirit in their lives.

This is a by-product of the Evangelistic Ministry, and we pray that this will be the situation throughout the present Mission.
In light of this, we regret that we must decline your invitation to him.
Yours Sincerely,
Maurice
L. Rowlandson
Director

بِسْمِ اللهِ الرَّحْمٰنِ الرَّحِيْمِ

The London Mosque

16 GRESSENHALL ROAD, LONDON SW18 5QL   TEL: 01-874 6298   CABLES: ISLAMABAD LONDON
01-874 7590
TELEX: 28604 MON REF. G1292

REF...... 4/7 ....   DATE 1.7.84
          3

پیارے عزیزم مطیع اللہ جی درد! ہرننگھم

السلام علیکم ورحمۃ اللہ وبرکاتہ

آپ کا خط بمعہ انٹرو لوکیٹ موصول ہوا۔ جزاکم اللہ تعالیٰ۔

اللہ تعالیٰ آپ کی تائید روح القدس سے فرمائے۔ آپ کی زبان، بیان اور تحریر میں تاثیر پیدا فرمائے۔ احمدیت کا نور پھیلانے میں فرشتوں کی مدد حاصل رہے۔

زندہ خدا اور زندہ نبی اور زندہ مسیح موعود اور زندہ قرآن کو پیش کرنا ہی احمدیت کا مقصد ہے۔ اللہ تعالیٰ آپ کو اس مقصد میں کامیاب و کامران کرے حق غالب آئے اور باطل مغلوب ہو۔

والسلام
نازلکم
خلیفۃ المسیح الرابع

Midland Tabligh Seminar

Ahmadiyya Muslim Association (UK) Central Tabligh Committee held a Tabligh seminar for the midlands at Birmingham on 13th July ,1986. I gave a lecture on the principle and importance of preaching. Dr Syed Farooq Ahmad spoke on ways and means of preaching and Mr. Muzzaffar Clarke spoke on "Why I accepted Ahmadiyyat". Maulana Ata-ul-Mujeeb Rashid, the Imam of the London Fazl Mosque gave the final address. Mr. Rafiq Ahmad Hayat the secretary of Tabligh UK thanked all the participants.

Mubahala Challenge

Molvi Mahmood Ahmad Mirpuri was editing 'Sirat e Mustaqeem', a monthly Urdu magazine from the Green Lane mosque in Birmingham. Once, a noted reporter of the Birmingham Evening Mail was going to write an article about the mosque. The reporter requested me to act as an interpreter. I helped the Molvis to translate into English whatever they said in response to the questions of the reporter. When the reporter had completed the interview the Molvis took the reporter to a side room in privacy. After a while the reporter came out and we both left. The reporter told me that the Molvis did not want my name to be included in the article because I was not a Muslim and the reporter was surprised at the ingratitude of the so called Molvis. They could have let my name be mentioned as an interpreter, not that I had any wish for my name to be in the article! Once in 'Sirat e Mustaqeem', in an editorial, a Qadiani Mudderis was warned not to tell his students about the Qadiani Ahmadiyya Teachings. I received a letter from one of the editors criticizing my Islamic explanation of the Prophet Hood of Hadhrat Krishna in India.

I had received a letter addressed to me as the president of the "Ahmadiyya Kafir Community" in the past, and I was well known as the Qadiani teacher and Kafir in the city. When the City of Birmingham Council was considering giving the old Tilton Road School to the Ahmadiyya Muslim Association in 1996, many non-Ahmadiyya Muslims and some of their organizations very strongly protested and petitioned the City Council. Some of my Students signed the petitions in the mosques and informed me of the frustration of their people. The non-Ahmadiyya Muslims were hoping to convince the City Council that Ahmadiyya Muslims were not Muslims; therefore, the listed building could not be given to the Ahmadies on the basis of Islam, as Ahmadies were declared non-Muslims by the

Government of Pakistan. Allah frustrated their plans, petitions and prayers. The City of Birmingham acted justly and treated the Birmingham Ahmadies equitably as any other citizen of any persuasion. It is not the duty of City Council to proclaim the religious beliefs or affiliations of its citizens. It is up to the citizens to declare or not to declare their beliefs themselves. This is guaranteed under the United Nations General Assembly Resolution 36/55 of 25th November 1981 S I-8.

No one has the right to force anyone to believe or not to believe. The choice rests with each human being.
"There is no compulsion in religion"
The Holy Quran- Chapter 2, Verse 257.

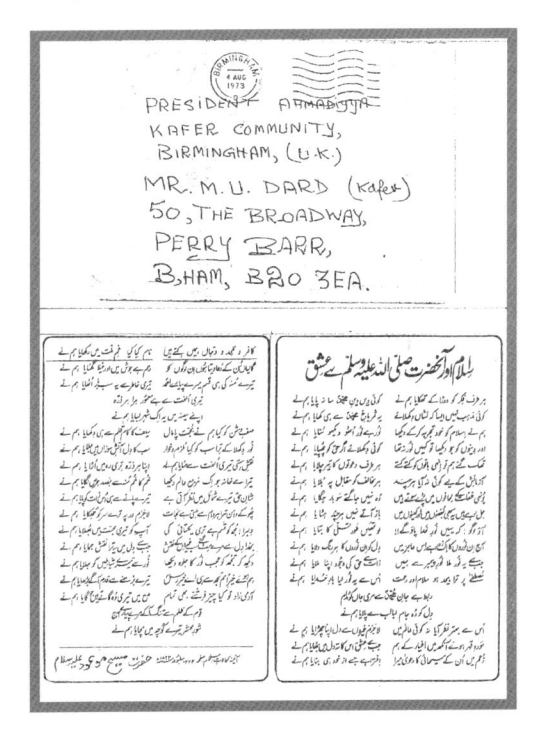

Many self appointed and so called leaders of the non Ahmadiyya Muslims continually complained against my teaching and interpretation of Islam to the Inspectors of the Local Education Authority and particularly to the Principals of the Joseph Chamberlain College. The Principals could not find any justification for the allegations against me. However, in 1997 the then Principle requested me to be more aware of the sensibilities of non-Ahmadiyya Muslims and to treat the Islamic content of the Advanced "A" level Urdu course with more impartiality.

An Ahmadiyya Muslim 67

I had always been mindful of presenting true and authentic Islam as portrayed by the great spiritual guides of the past fourteen centuries and universally accepted by the majority of Muslims around the world. I made sure that all shades of opinion and differing interpretations were put before my students. Whenever they asked questions and initiated the discussions in the class; I remained impartial.

Molvi Mahmood Ahmad Mirpuri issued a statement warning and condemning Hadhrat Mirza Tahir Ahmad, Khalifatul Masih IV, Supreme Head of the Ahmadiyya Muslims in the 'Daily Millat', an Urdu newspaper in London dated 7th September 1988. He said that when King Faisal, Bhutto and Gen. Zia were killed, the Ahmadies claimed their deaths in response to the prayer challenge given by Ahmadies. In fact he himself had accepted the challenge by making this statement, and within a few weeks the wrath of Allah pounced on him. He was killed in a car accident on the M6, and while his dead body lay in the house, a ceiling fell down and injured the mourners. Hadhrat Mirza Tahir Ahmad Khalifatul Masih IV wrote to me in his letter of the 15th October 1988 that "One enemy of the Ahmadiyyat has fallen a prey to Mubahala here as well. Would that people take heed from these lesson-teaching signs and derive benefit from the light of Ahmadiyyat!"

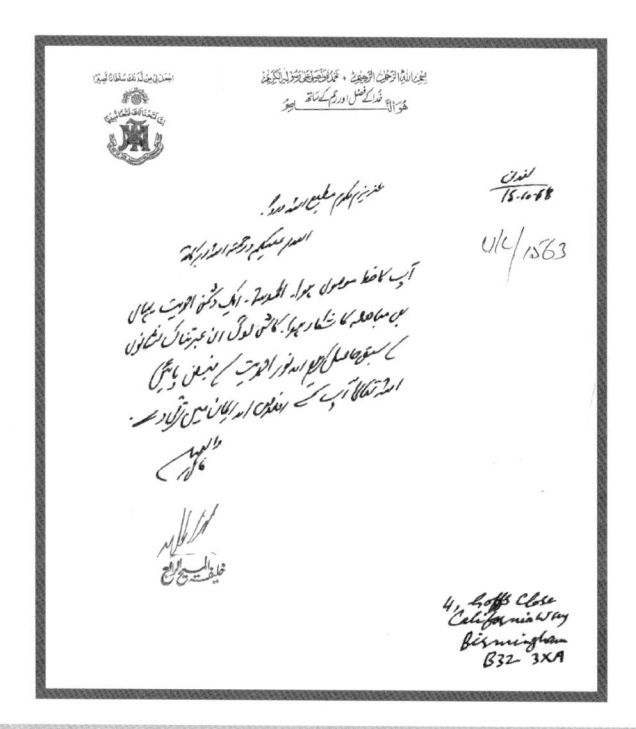

Office Bearers of the Ahmadiyya Muslim Association of Birmingham 1973-1974

President	Matiullah Dard.
General Secretary	Nasir Wasim Ward.
Finance Secretary	Abdul Hafeez
Education Secretary	Rashid Ahmad
Preaching Secretary	Matiullah Dard
Tehrik Jadid Secretary	Abdul Wase Adam Chughtai

Office Bearers of the Ahmadiyya Muslim Association of Birmingham 1974-1975

President	Matiullah Dard
General Secretary	Nasir Ahmad Mubashar
Education Secretary	Rashid Ahmad
Finance Secretary	Abdul Hafeez
Preaching Secretary	Matiullah Dard

Office Bearers of the Ahmadiyya Muslim Association of Birmingham 1975

President	Abdul Hafeez
General Secretary	Muhammad Iqbal Dar
Finance Secretary	Matiullah Dard
Education Secretary	Rashid Ahmad
Preaching Secretary	Matiullah Dard.

Bait in Birmingham

Dar-ul-Barakat

In 1980 a property was bought at 792, Washwood Health Road, B8 2JL. It was named "Dar-ul-Barakat" and was used as our centre and mosque. Mr. Nasim Ahmad Bajwa was appointed as Regional Missionary resident at the centre. He is an experienced and astute preacher who organised the community on progressive lines.

Hadhrat Mirza Tahir Ahmad was elected Khalifatul Masih IV in 1982 when Hadhrat Mirza Nasir Ahmad, Khalifatul Masih III passed away in Pakistan. Soon after Khalifatul Masih IV visited Birmingham and we had the good fortune to renew our oath of allegiance on his hands. He addressed the Ahmadiyya community at the George Cadbury Hall in Birmingham. A reception was held in his honour at the Strathallan Thistle Hotel on the Hagley Road, where the distinguished citizens of Birmingham had a chance to meet him.

Hadhrat Mirza Tahir Ahmad Khalifatul Masih IV accompanied by Matiullah Dard arriving at George Cadbury Hall Birmingham.

Matiullah Dard calling Adhan in Cadbury Hall Birmingham

Nazim Dar-ul-Barakat

The regional Committee of the Midlands presided over by Mr. N. A. Bajwa appointed me as the Nazim-Dar-ul-Barakat on the 30th August, 1982. My responsibilities were defined by the committee as follows:
1- To look after and maintain the centre.
2- To organize prayers, Dars and supervise the use of the premises in the absence of the Missionary.
3- To assist the Missionary to facilitate the work of the community.

I looked after the centre for a couple of months until Mirza Naseer Ahmad was appointed. Malik Nisar Ahmad, Hospitality Secretary opened and closed the centre daily. The Nazim was deeply grateful for his assistance. A welcome meeting was held on the 11th November 1982 chaired by Mr. N. A. Bajwa at the centre, Dar-ul-Barakat. Mr Abdul Ghafoor, President Leamington Spa and Coventry welcomed Mirza Naseer Ahmad and I bade farewell to Mr. Nasim Ahmad Bajwa. I thanked him for his guidance and help. Mr. N. A. Bajwa was transferred to Southall Ahmadiyya centre.

We held monthly meetings, seminars, all congregational prayers, preaching meetings and special occasions were celebrated at Dar-ul-Barakat. All the affiliated organisations of Ahmadiyya men, women and children held their respective meetings and prize distributions, sometimes in the presence of distinguished visitors from London, at Dar-ul-Barakat.

M. A. Psychology Final Year Students Govt. College Lahore 1957

Mirza Naseer Ahmad was an effective, kind, hospitable and popular regional missionary among the youth of the community particularly. Mirza Mahmood Ahmad and Maulana Ghulam Ahmad Khadim have also worked here as regional missionaries. All through the 1980's and 1990's Dar-ul-Barakat remained the hub of Ahmadiyya Muslim activities. I am sure that Mr. Abdul Hafeez, Mr. Muhammad Ilyas khan and Dr. Syed Farooq Ahmad the past presidents, would have recorded the important events during their own term of office. Dr. Muhammad Ashraf the current President has asked me to undertake the writing of this early history of Birmingham. In obedience to his bidding I have mentioned only those facts and events in which I was personally involved as the preaching secretary and the Chairman of the Preaching Committee. I might have missed or forgotten something for which I crave the reader's indulgence and forgiveness. I am not a historian and have completed this task only to obey the administration of Khilafat-e-Ahmadiyya and to please Allah alone. I am acutely aware of my inabilities and shortcomings. I do not wish to claim credit where credit is not due! May Allah forgive me for any mistakes, unintentionally committed, during this writing. Amin.

I retired from part time lectureship in April 1999, however, I have willingly and happily accepted the responsibilities of Waqf-e-Nau, Talim and Tarbiyyat Secretary of the Ahmadiyya Muslim Association, Birmingham. In 1997 Allah blessed us with the gift of spacious school building and the land. The school, once a ruin, is being restored by the Birmingham Ahmadiyya Muslim Association to its Victorian splender. The old Tilton Road school has now become the Dar-ul-Barakat Mosque and Community Centre. I pray that it will continue to serve as the "House of Blessings" for many generations of Ahmadies to come, Insha'Allah, The building was founded in 1889 which is exactly the same year that the Promised Messiah initiated the Ahmadiyya Muslim Movement in Ludhiana, India,, Like him, we too found severe opposition from the non-Ahmadi Muslims but justice and fair play won the day and their opposition melted away like dew in the sunshine, but we are always watchful.
On the 7th February, 1999 I was visiting the new centre when to my surprise (and I must admit, to my delight also), I was asked to preside over the First Monthly Meeting to be held there.

Millennibrum

– bringing Birmingham's history to life

Millennibrum

Millennibrum Project
Birmingham Central Library
Chamberlain Square
Birmingham B3 3HQ
Tel: 0121-~~303 2657~~ 464 0576
Fax: 0121-464 0580
E-mail: millennibrum@birmingham.gov.uk
Website: www.millennibrum.org

12 September 2000

Dear Mr Dard,

I know that you are planning to move to Belgium, if you have not already left Birmingham, so I hope I am able to reach you before you go. I have tried to reach you by telephone but without success so far.

I am writing to seek your permission to compose a short article on your life and work in Birmingham for one of the forthcoming supplements the Millennibrum Project is producing for the Evening Mail or Birmingham Post to coincide with Black History Month in October. I would use material from your book and the interview that Lorraine Blakemore conducted with you. If I am not able to make contact with you before you receive this letter could you give me a telephone call?

On behalf of the Project I would like to thank you for your outstanding support for our activities. You have been one of the key contributors to Birmingham's recent history and I am delighted that we now have a detailed record for current and future generations, of your role in enhancing the political, educational and religious life of the City.

My very best wishes for the future.

Yours sincerely,

Malcolm Dick

Malcolm Dick
Editor

– bringing Birmingham's history to life

DIGITAL MEDIA CENTRE
UCE
Birmingham Institute Of Art and Design
Gosta Green
Corporation St
B4 7DX
TEL – 0121 331 7819
Fax – 0121 333 6020
e-mail – videobrum@hotmail.com

Millennibrum

Date 24/10/00

Dear Matiullah Dard

Thank you so much for your help and participation in the Millennibrum Project, filmed on the 6th September 2000, 85 Tilton Rd. It was a great success.

The intention of the Project is to record life as it is, in Birmingham in the year 2000, covering a complete cross section of the community. These recordings will be preserved permanently as part of the City's archives and will be available for use by members of the public on the premise of the City Council. Some will go onto the Millennibrum website and CD-ROM.

The tape will be available for viewing on the 6th floor, archive department, of the Central Library, Febuary/March 2001.

Hopefully the recordings of the Ahmadia Muslims will not only be of great use to researchers in the future, but also for the next and forthcoming generations of the Ahmadia community.

Yours sincerely,

Tom Ambler

An Ahmadiyya Muslim

– bringing Birmingham's history to life

DIGITAL MEDIA CENTRE
UCE
Birmingham Institute Of Art and Design
Gosta Green
Corporation St
B4 7DX
TEL – 0121 331 7819
Fax – 0121 333 6020
e-mail – videobrum@hotmail.com

Millennibrum

Date 24/10/00

Dear Matiullah Dard

Thank you so much for your help and participation in the Millennibrum Project, filmed on the 6th September 2000, 85 Tilton Rd. It was a great success.

The intention of the Project is to record life as it is, in Birmingham in the year 2000, covering a complete cross section of the community. These recordings will be preserved permanently as part of the City's archives and will be available for use by members of the public on the premise of the City Council. Some will go onto the Millennibrum website and CD-ROM.

The tape will be available for viewing on the 6th floor, archive department, of the Central Library, Febuary/March 2001.

Hopefully the recordings of the Ahmadia Muslims will not only be of great use to researchers in the future, but also for the next and forthcoming generations of the Ahmadia community.

Yours sincerely,

Tom Ambler

Eight Videos made by;

1) Maulana Nasim Ahmad Bajwa- Regional Missionary
2) Dr. Mubasher Ahmad Salim
3) Dr. Mohammad Ashraf
4) Mr. Adam Abdul wasi Chughtai
5) Mr. M. Clarke
6) Matiullah Dard
7) Wajeeha Bajwa
8) Sophia Anwar

M
A Millennium Commission
Lottery Project

UCE
Birmingham

Birmingham Post
& Mail Group

MILLENNIUM
2000
Birmingham City Council

An Ahmadiyya Muslim 75

An Ahmadiyya Muslim 76

Chairman

Maulana Laeeq Ahmad Tahir informed me on the 3rd October, 2000 that I had been appointed a member of the Syllabus of English committee of the Jamia Ahmadiyya International by the Amir UK.

The Jamia will be established in 2003 at Bait ul Futuh, Morden. The first meeting of the committee was held at Dar us Salam Southall on Saturday the 18th November, 2000. Maulana Laeeq Ahmad Tahir, the Principal designate, guided us and explained the objectives of the Committee. I was elected as the chairman of the committee inspite of my protestation. The committee was entrusted to devise a syllabus of English to develop the oral, aural, reading and writing skills of the students, so that they can deliver sermons, preach and discourse in English effectively and convincingly. My colleagues and I discussed the various General Certificate of English Advanced level syllabi of a few examination boards. Our deliberation continued until evening and it was decided to hold the next meeting on the 20th January, 2001 at Bait ul Futuh, Morden. We hope to complete our work soon, Inshallah.

Postscript

All knowing Allah, I am your most insignificant servant. You know all my sins, vices and blunders. I am indebted to your limitless forgiveness, and yoked by my innumerable deficiencies and mistakes. Your Blessings are infinite, and my wrong doings are incalculable.

All my faculties are your gifts, all the facilities are provided by you, and all the opportunities to serve are created by you. All my talents to utilize these opportunities are given to me by you. My birth, parents, upbringing, family, friends and to be at the right place at the right time, are designed and executed by you. You have manifested the Right Path for me.

> Although through life I have
> Ever been a target broad
> For fortune's freaks;
> But wrapped in this
> Or lost in that
> Though stumbling, falling,
> Staggering on, in every stress
> Of pain and pleasure,
> My fondest and obedient thoughts
> Have always turned to Thee- My Lord

You imbued the love of the "Seal of the Prophets" in my heart and mind. You inculcated the love of the Promised Messiah in me during my childhood.

> Well and truly have I
> Tasted of the joys of life
> Through drinking deep
> At the fountain of Love:
> Indeed I have felt a pain
> Which knows no cure,
> And found a balm
> Which cures all pain!

You blessed me through the prayers of Hadhrat Mirza Bashir ul Din Mahmood Ahmad Khalifatul Masih II, Hadhrat Mirza Nasir Ahmad Khalifatul Masih III, Hadhrat Mirza Tahir Ahmad Khalifatul Masih IV, and many distinguished companions of the Promised Messiah throughout my career. You gave me life at Qadian, trained me at Rabwah, and guided me in Fiji, New Zealand and the United Kingdom. If I have been able to do any good of any kind, anywhere, at any time, it has been achieved only through your blessing and inexhaustible mercy.

I penned it only to please you my Allah

"*And the bounty of the Lord proclaim*" The Holy Quran- Chapter 93, verse 12

All praise belongs to Allah

Matiullah Dard
"Peace",
4, Goffs Close,
California Way,
Harborne Rise,
Birmingham
B32 3XA
15th June 1999

Hadhrat Khalifatul Masih III (rh) in London 1967

An Ahmadiyya Muslim 78

My Life as a Senior Citizen

I sold my house in Birmingham in 2001 and moved to Belgium to live with my son in Waterloo. Every Friday I went to the Ahmadiyya Mission House and Mosque in Dilbeek, near Brussels for my JUMMA Prayers. The Amir Jama'at Syed Hamid Mahmood Shah and the Missionary very kindly provided opportunities for preaching Ahmadiyyat. Syed Hamid Mahmood Shah Sahib included me in the team which was being interviewed on the Local Belgian Television Channel about Ahmadiyyat. I spoke in English and the Interviewer translated it in French. My son found another better job and moved to the U S A. I went back to the U K. I have been living in Woolwich Arsenal, since, April, 2003. I became a member of the South East London Ahmadiyya Jama'at and was appointed as a Secretary Foreign Affairs of the Community.

The MERCURY WEEKLY published the news of the inauguration of " **Bait- ul- Futuh Mosque**" with my interview and a photo with Hadhoor. The excerpt of this news of the Mercury has been included in the Film/Documentary Video of the Ahmadiyya Muslim Association called " One Community, One Leader " telecast on the Muslim Television Ahmadiyya. I was appointed as the Secretary General of the South East London Ahmadiyya Muslim Association in 2004. I have been giving lectures on Islam in many primary and secondary schools in the South East London area, organised by the Bexley and Thamesmead Multi-Faith Forums. I have been serving the Forums as the Vice-Chairman, since, December, 2008. I had an (heart- by-pass) operation in December,2006 in a London hospital. After a week I was sent for two weeks in a Convalescence Home, near the beach in Brighton. The South East London Ahmadiyya Jama'at looked after me by providing cooked meals for a week when I came back to London. May Allah reward and bless them all for their generosity, amen. The South East London Ahmadiyya Jama'at covered a vast area of five boroughs of London. I suggested that this very large Jama'at should be divided into four smaller Jama'ats, but the people at the helm of affairs decided to split it into two Jama'ats; Bromley & Lewisham Jama'at and Bexley & Greenwich Jama'at. The election/consultation of the two new Jama'ats were held on the 18th April, 2010 under the supervision of the Regional Amir Mr Naseem Afzal Butt. The new approved office-bearers will assume their responsibilities on the 1st of July, 2010. I am a member of the newly formed Bexley & Greenwich Ahmadiyya Muslim Jama'at. I have been appointed as the Vice President and Talim & Tarbiyyat Secretary of the new Jama'at.

Matiullah Dard at Minaratul Masih, Qadian 1973

Miscellanies

The Promised Messiah & Imam Mahdi Alaihisslam
By Matiullah Dard

Muhammad bin Ali (Imam Muhammad Baqir) relates that the Holy Prophet (Peace be upon him) said:
"Surely two signs will appear for our Mahdi which have never appeared before (as signs of truth for anyone else), since the creation of heaven and earth. In the month of Ramzan, the moon will be eclipsed on the first of its nights, (of eclipse), and the sun will be eclipsed on the middle day (of its days of eclipse). Both these eclipses will take place in the same month of Ramzan. And these two signs have never occurred before since Allah created the heavens and the earth." (Sunnan Dar Qutni; Vol. 1)

In this Hadith the two greatest signs of true Imam Mahdi are mentioned with the following details:

(i) After the claim of Imam Mahdi two signs will appear.
(ii) The moon will be eclipsed on the 13th of Ramadhan, which is the first night of the 3 nights of lunar eclipses.
(iii) The sun will be eclipsed on the 28th day of Ramadhan, which is the middle day of the 3 days of solar eclipses.
(iv) Both signs will appear in the same Ramadhan.
(v) These signs have never appeared for anyone except the true Mahdi

Eclipses

Eclipses of the moon are governed by the Law of Physics. The moon is eclipsed when the shadow of the earth falls on it and this will happen when the earth is between the sun and the moon. Thus, it can only occur during full moon. According to astronomers, therefore, a lunar eclipse can occur on the 13th, 14th and 15th day of the dates of the Muslim calendar. Known as the Hijri Qamri Calendar and each month begins with sightings of the new Moon. The solar eclipse occurs when the Moon intervenes the Earth and the Sun and the three are in one straight line. This can happen on the 27th, 28th and 29th only of the Muslim month. Hence, the Prophecy demanded that the lunar eclipse should occur on the first of the three possible nights i.e. on the 13th and the solar eclipse to happen on the middle of three possible dates i.e. on the 28th. Both eclipses had to take place during the month of Ramadhan and at a time when someone was claiming to be the Mahdi.

Thus when, in 1891 and under divine direction, Hadhrat Mirza Ghulam Ahmad of Qadian claimed to be the Messiah and Mahdi, opponents demanded that the heavenly sign of the eclipses be shown and since this had not been observed his claim could not be taken seriously.
However, since Allah had appointed Hadhrat Mirza Ghulam Ahmad, he was also going to establish his truth. Thus in precise accordance of the requirements of the Prophecy of the Holy Prophet Muhammad (May Allah's peace and blessings be upon him) these eclipses were witnessed in 1894 A.D. the lunar month of Ramadhan began on the 9th March and ended on the 6th April,1894.

On the 13th of Ramzan (21st March 1894 AD) a partial eclipse of the Moon was observed. This was followed on the 28th of the same month (5th April 1894 AD) with a solar eclipse of the annular type. These eclipses were widely visible all over India and in many other countries of the world in the Eastern Hemisphere. During the following year the Lunar month of Ramadhan began on the 26th February and ended on the 26th March 1895. A similar set of eclipses was witnessed on the Western Horizon on the 10th March and 25th March 1895 (13th Ramadhan and 28th Ramadhan)

On the appearance of this sign, Hazrat Mirza Ghulam Ahmad presented it to the world at large and in particular to the opposing Muslim divines as a prophecy fulfilled in his favour. He wrote a book entitled Noor-ul-Haq (Part two published in May 1894) discussing the detailed implication of the Prophecy. Several thousand responded to this news by entering the fold of Ahmadiyyat.
This is a unique sign. If we scan through history never have such eclipses occurred during the month of Ramzan and never at a time when someone has claimed to be the Mahdi. It is one very special sign that points to the veracity of the claim of Hazrat Mirza Ghulam Ahmad.

The grand manifestation which is beyond human intervention of any kind calls for serious reflection. In one aspect it was a manifestation which was determined by the law governing the movement of the planet, and there was no room in it for human intervention; yet in another aspect it was a magnificent sign in support of the truth of the Holy Prophet, peace be upon him. He could not have known or guessed that such a manifestation would take place 1260 years after his death. Even if such a manifestation had occurred just by itself, its prediction twelve and half centuries earlier would have been conclusive proof of the truth of the Holy Prophet, peace be upon him.

But it did not stand alone. It had another splendid and glorious aspect. Its occurrence was to serve as a warning that the Mahdi had appeared and that those who were awaiting his advent, should _seek him, accept him and obey him._ So that they might thus participate in the glorious revival of Islam which God had decreed would be achieved through that devoted servant of the Holy Prophet, peace be on him, who had led a pure and blameless life in accord with the teachings of Islam, and who was a constant recipient of divine revelation, had under divine command, proclaimed that he was the Mahdi, the manifestation would be hailed as a conclusive and glorious confirmation of the truth of the Holy Prophet, peace be on him, and of such a claimant and of Islam.

Hazrat Mirza Ghulam Ahmad of Qadian India, who was born on 20th February 1835, and died on the 26th May,1908, began to receive divine revelation around 1876 and continued to receive it with greater and greater frequency throughout the rest of his life. In 1878-1882 he wrote his epoch-making book Braheen - e - Ahmadiyya in which he demonstrated completely the superiority of Islam over other faiths in such a manner that he was unanimously acclaimed by the leading contemporary Muslim divines of India as the greatest champion of Islam. Although true Prophets and claimants have always shown thousands of signs to prove their truth, a single sign should be enough for a sincere person. The glorious sign of the promised eclipses for the Promised Messiah and Mahdi is one such sign which should not pass any sincere person without convincing him. Mention to this extraordinary sign can also be found in the New Testament to mark the second coming of Jesus. The gospel according to Matthew states: "*Immediately after the tribulations of those days, shall the sun be darkened and the moon shall not give her light and the stars shall fall from heaven; and the powers of the heavens shall be shaken. And then shall appear the sign of the son of man in heaven.*" (24:29-30)

The gospel of St. Mark (13:24) says: "*But in those days, after the tribulation, the sun shall be darkened, and the moon shall not give her light and the stars shall be falling from heaven and the power that are in the heavens shall be shaken. And then shall they see the Son of Man coming in clouds with great power and glory.*" Eclipses have no doubt occurred before but never as a sign of the advent of a heavenly reformer; because there has never been in the history of the world a claimant of any kind at the time of the Phenomena described.

It is obvious that these words cannot be taken literally. If the sun were to be really darkened, life on this planet would become extinct, as all life is dependent on the light of the sun. If the stars fell from the heavens, this universe would be annihilated; for every part of the universe is dependent upon the other and cannot exist without it. Again, if the power of Heaven were shaken literally, not only men but even angels would cease to exist. Jesus himself has said that after these things come to pass, the son of man will take away the Earth from the evil doers and give the inheritance to the righteous would become impossible.
It is clear, therefore, that the Prophecy cannot be constructed literally and that there is a hidden meaning in it, as is very often the case with revealed words; and

that meaning is that the sun and the moon will be eclipsed in those days and meteors will fall in large numbers, and the power of religious leaders over their followers will be weakened, for in religious literature heavenly powers-sun, moon and stars- signify leaders of religion, who "Shine as lights in the world." (Phil. 2:15)

Harmsworth's Universal Encyclopaedia says under Andromedids (remains of the Biela-coment):
"*There were notable showers in 1872, 1885 and 1892.*" It was witnessed by the Promised Messiah Hazrat Ahmad himself and God told him at that time that it was a sign of his advent.

These signs appear at first sight to be very common ones, for solar and lunar eclipses and the falling of meteors are no extraordinary Phenomena, and the power of religious leaders has often been shaken before. But on reflection it would appear that these are mighty signs, for although details are not given in the Gospels, these having been compiled a considerable time after Jesus, Islamic traditions specify, a limitation concerning those eclipses which invest them with peculiar value as signs indicating the period when the Messiah would re-appear. These signs were fulfilled in 1894 in the Eastern hemisphere, and in 1895 in the Western Hemisphere, so that the whole world became its witness, for confirmation please see the letter of the Royal Observatory Greenwich addressed to me appended.

(An abridged version of this essay was also published in the First Promised Messiah Edition Magazine "Ansaruddin" of the Majlis Ansarullah U K March, 2004 Entitled "Heavenly Signs of the Mahdi")

Lord Avebury Presiding a meeting in House of Lords discussing Human Rights with members of Ahamdiyya Jama'at

Royal Observatory Greenwich

ROYAL OBSERVATORY GREENWICH

Matiullah Dard
Education Secretary
Ahmadiyya Muslim Association
Dar-ul-Barakat Mosque
85 Tilton Road
Birmingham
B9 4PP

5th May 2000

Dear Mr. Dard,

Below is the eclipse data you requested. If you have any further questions regarding the data feel free to contact me again.

Eclipses of the Sun and Moon as seen from the Eastern Hemisphere, 1894:

- The Moon was eclipsed on 20th/21st March
- The Sun was eclipsed on 5th April
- The Lunar Month began on 9th March and ended on the 6th April

Eclipses of the Sun and Moon as seen from the Western Hemisphere, 1895:

- The Moon was eclipsed on 10th March
- The Sun was eclipsed on 25th March
- The Lunar Month began on the 26th February and ended 26th March

Yours sincerely,

Rob Warren
Assistant Astronomy Officer
Royal Observatory, Greenwich
Direct Line: +44 (0)20 8312 6568
Fax: +44 (0)20 8312 6734
E-mail: rwarren@nmm.ac.uk

Royal Observatory Greenwich, London SE10 9NF
Tel: 0181 312 6575 Fax: 0181 312 6771 www.rog.nmm.ac.uk
National Maritime Museum, Royal Observatory Greenwich, Queen's House

GREENWICH MERIDIAN 2000

An Ahmadiyya Muslim

Mr. Robert Massey
The Astronomer
Royal Observatory,
Greenwich, London SE 10 9NF

Matiullah Dard
Foreign Affairs Secretary
South East London
Ahmadiyya Muslim Community
126 Hill View Drive
Thamesmead West
London SE 28 0LJ

23/02/04

Dear Mr. Massey,

I would be most grateful of you could confirm as an astronomer the following four facts: **A, B, C and D,** about the eclipses of the Sun and the Moon.

A The solar eclipses occur when the Moon intervenes the earth and the Sun and the three are in one straight line. This can happen only on the 27th, 28th and 29th of the Lunar month of the Lunar calendar.

B The Moon is eclipsed when the shadow of the Earth falls on it, and this will happen when the Earth is between the sun and the Moon. Thus, it can only occur during a full Moon. According to Astronomers, therefore, a Lunar eclipse can occur only on the 13th, 14th, and 15th day of the dates of the Lunar month of the Lunar calendar. Each Lunar month begins with the sighting of the new Moon.

C Eclipses of the Sun and the Moon as seen from the Eastern Hemisphere in 1894

1. The Moon was eclipsed on the 20th and 21st March

2. The Sun was eclipsed on the 5th April

3. The Lunar month began on the 9th March and ended on the 6th April.

D Eclipses of the Sun and the Moon as seen from the Western Hemisphere in 1895

1. The Moon was eclipsed on the 10th March

2. The Sun was eclipsed on the 25th March

3. The Lunar month began on the 26th February and ended on the 26th March

Yours Sincerely

M. Dard

M. Dard

NATIONAL MARITIME MUSEUM **ROYAL OBSERVATORY GREENWICH**

...illustrating the importance of the sea, ships, time and the stars...

Matiullah Dard,   10th May 2004
Foreign Affairs Secretary,
Ahmadiyya Muslim South East London Community,
126 Hill View Drive,
Thamesmead West,
London SE28 0LJ

Dear Mr. Dard,

Thank you for your letter of 23rd February.

In reply to your enquiry: the facts you quote in paragraphs A and B are essentially correct. For a full explanation, I suggest you refer to the Explanatory Supplement to the Astronomical Almanac, ISBN 0-935702-68-7.

As far as paragraphs C and D are concerned: we do not have details of past eclipses to hand. I suggest that you access the website of Fred Espanak : www.mreclipse.com
for enquiries of this nature.

I hope that this information is of some help to you.

Yours sincerely,

A.J.Sizer

A.J.Sizer

Patron: HRH The Duke of Edinburgh, KG, KT
National Maritime Museum, Greenwich, London SE10 9NF
Tel: 020 8858 4422 Fax: 020 8312 6632 www.nmm.ac.uk

An Ahmadiyya Muslim   87

Hadhrat Maulana Abdul-Raheem Dard (ra)
By Prof. Matiullah Dard
Vice-Chairman, Bexley and Thamesmead Multi-Faith Forms London

He was born on the 19th June, 1894 at Ludhiana in India. He was the eldest son of Hadhrat Master Qadir Bakhsh, one of the three hundred and thirteen chosen companions of the Promised Messiah Hadhrat Mirza Ghulam Ahmad. Hadhrat Molvi Abdullah Sanauri, an eye witness of the miracle of Red Drops, enjoys a unique status in the history of Ahmadiyyat was his uncle. Hadhrat A.R Dard was brought up in the spiritual atmosphere of the Promised Messiah and his companions. He listened and memorised many of the sayings of the Promised Messiah and thus earned the distinction to be called a companion of the Promised Messiah and Imam Mahdi Alaihissalam. He followed the footsteps of his father and uncle who were mentioned with love and affection in glowing terms by the Promised Messiah in his book Izala-e-Auham. Maulana A.R Dard spent all his life in the service of Islam. He was one of the distinguished and noted early devotees of the early period of the Second Khilafat-e- Ahmadiyya. He served Islam and Ahmadiyyat with righteous steadfastness and prominence until his death that future generations will be proud of his selfless contributions in the renaissance of the Islamic Culture and Civilization. After obtaining his Master Of Arts degree, he was offered a post of a sub-judge, but he rejected this offer and prefered the life of a poor missionary of Islam. Mr. Muhammad Muneer the Chief Justice Of Pakistan was his class-fellow and used to say, "had my friend not gone astray (he meant discarding the worldly wealth and accepting willingly the poor life style of a Muslim missionary) Mr. Dard would have been the Chief Justice Of Pakistan instead of me".

For eight years he preached Islam, successfully in the U.K. and other European Countries (Holland, Belgium, Albania and Spain) and set an excellent example of serving Islam. In 1924 Hadhrat Musleh Maud Mirza Bashir-Ud-Din Mahmood Ahmad laid the foundation stone of the very first Muslim Mosque in London and appointed Hadhrat A. R. Dard as its First Imam. He supervised the completion of this Historic Mosque in two years. The opening ceremony of the Fazal Mosque in October, 1926 was an extra ordinary and unusual event in the history of London which was covered by the London Press and the world media for many days. God Almighty had ordained the blessing of building of the very First Mosque by Muslims in the U.K. under the supervision of Hadhrat Dard as its First Imam. This Mosque has a unique importance in the History of Ahmadiyyat. It became the center of activities of Hadhrat Mirza Tahir Ahmad, Khalifa tul Masih 1V in April,1984 after his miraculous escape and migration from Pakistan. In April, 2003, the Historic Election of Hadhrat Mirza Masroor Ahmad, Khalifa tul Masih V took place in this Blessed Mosque for the First time in the history of

Ahmadiyya Movement outside Rabwah and Qadian.

Hadhrat Maulana Dard came as a Private Secretary and one of the Twelve Chosen Disciples of Hadhrat Musleh Maud in 1924 and remained the Ahmadiyya Muslim Missionary in-charge of the U.K and the Imam of the Fazal Mosque, London until 1928. He worked tirelessly to enhance the Prestige of the Ahmadiyya Movement and established useful contacts in the intellectual and political circles of London. He went back to India and served as a Nazir (secretary) of various departments. His services as a foreign affairs secretary were applauded particularly by Hadhrat Musleh Maud. He was also appointed as an additional Nazir-Ala (Chief Secretary). He worked as a member of the Board of Translators of the Holy Quran with Hadhrat Mirza Bashir Ahmad, Hadhrat Maulana Sher Ali and others.

In 1931, All India Kashmir Committee was formed under the Presidency of Hadhrat Musleh Maud to release the Muslims of Kashmir from the bondage and yoke of the tyrant Raja and Hadhrat A. R. Dard was appointed as the Secretary of the Committee. He was also a member of the All India Muslim League for sometime. He was not only a Muslim Missionary but also rendered valuable services for the Indian Muslims in the political field. His services are amply recorded in the History of Kashmir. Sheikh Muhammad Abdullah, the Lion of Kashmir, had mentioned the services of the President and the Secretary of the All India Kashmir Committee in his letters, as well, which he wrote to Musleh Maud in appreciation of Ahmadi volunteers in Kashmir.

In February, 1933 Hadhrat Dard was appointed the Imam of the Fazl Mosque London for the second time. He was entrusted by Hadhrat Musleh Maud with a special mission in London. It was to persuade and convince Mr. Muhammad Ali Jinnah to change his mind and return to India to lead the Muslims of the Sub-continent. Quaid- i-Azam Mr M.A Jinnah had become disgusted with the Indian Political scene so much so, that he had decided to live and Practice, Permanently in London after attending the Round Table conferences held by the British Government. Sir Muhammad Zafrullah Khan writes about Hadhrat Maulana Dard's contribution in his book, Ahmadiyyat- the Re-naissance of Islam, "By 1933 Hadhrat Khalifa tul Masih was so distressed at the Prospect that face the Muslims in India that he felt very strongly that a person of the political sagacity and iron nerve of Mr. Jinnah was needed to secure for the Muslims a decent Political future in India. He, therefore, directed Mr. A. R. Dard, Imam of London Mosque, to get in touch with Mr. Jinnah and try to persuade him to return to India and take up, and fight for, the cause of the Muslims. Mr. Dard called on Mr. Jinnah and had a long talk with him. He found that the task assigned to him by the Khalifa tul Masih was a very uphill one. Mr. Jinnah was most reluctant, but eventually changed his mind and agreed to return to India and to Place himself at the head of the Political struggle of the Muslims for safeguarding their position in an independent India. Mr. Jinnah was approached from time to time by certain leading figures among the Muslims of India who also urged him to return to India. But, there can be no doubt that what prevailed with him in the end was the persistence of Mr. Dard under the directions of the Khalifa tul Masih. When Mr. Jinnah intimated his willingness to return to India Mr. Dard held a reception in his honour at the London Mosque which was very well attended. Mr. Jinnah addressed the gathering on India of the future. He started with the announcement that Mr. Dard's persuasion had compelled him to enter the political field again from which he had withdrawn sometime back. He said: "The eloquent persuasion of the Imam left me no way of escape". His speech was widely reported. The Sunday Times, London, wrote in its issue of 9April, 1933". There was a large gathering in the grounds of the mosque in Melrose Road, Wimbledon, where Mr. Jinnah the famous Indian Muslim, Spoke on India's future. Mr. Jinnah made unfavorable comments on the Indian White Paper from a national point of view. The chairman, Sir Nairn Stewart Sandeman M.P. tool up the Churchill attitude on the subject, and this led to heckling by some of the Muslim students, who were, however, eventually calmed by the Imam of the Mosque".

The very first Muslim newspaper in London, 'The Muslim Times' was Published in 1935 under the editorship of the Maulana A.R. Dard. He also edited the 'Review of Religious' in London from 1924 to 1928 and Hadhrat Mirza Bashir Ahmad was the co-editor at Qadian. Allah had blessed him in his scholarly research which he carried out along with his secretarial and other responsibilities by producing the first biography in English Language of the Promised Messiah entitled 'Life Of Ahmad'. He also wrote 'Islamic Khilafat' in English, An exalted position of the Muslim Woman, in Urdu, The Hadees, in English and The History of Spain. An 'Islamic Album' was published in London in 1936. He delivered a speech on ' The Founder of the Ahmadiyya Movement and English People" at an annual gathering in Rabwah. This speech was published in the book. Hadhrat Syed Waliullah Shah translated this very important book into The Arabic Language, in order to counter-balance the anti-Ahmadiyya propaganda in the Arabic speaking countries. This book refutes with cogent arguments that the Ahmadiyya Movement was created by the British.

When my Uncle Hadhrat Chaudhary Fateh Muhammad Sial bought the piece of land at Putney In London in 1920, Hadhrat Musleh Maud was staying at Dalhousie Hill Station In India .This news pleased him so much that he arranged a feast to celebrate this purchase of Land and during the feast many people recited Poems. Hadhrat A.R. Dard was known as Molvi Rahim Baksh at that time, since his birth. Hadhrat Musleh Maud was very pleased with the recitation of a Poem by Molvi Raheem Baksh that he decided to change his name to Abdul Raheem and gave him the title DARD as a special name Since , 1920 he is known as Maulana Abdul Raheem Dard. Many a traditions were reported in the 'Seera tul Mahdi' written by Hadhrat Mirza Bashir Ahmad with the words, Molvi Rahim

Baksh, M.A narrated.

Hadhrat Mirza Bashir Ahmad states that when in Feburary,1944 Hadhrat Musleh Maud celebrated the announcement of him being the Musleh Maud at Hoshiar Pur in the special meeting and the subsequent meetings held at Lahore, Ludhiana and Delhi, Maulana Dard was especially selected to read the 'Prophecy Concerning The Promised Son' because his uncle Hadhrat Munshi Abdullah Sanauri was a chosen companion of the Promised Messiah during the 'Chilla'- The Forty Days Of Prayers and meditation of the Promised Messiah in seclusion, when he received the revelation about Musleh Maud. This tradition has been continued in the Ahmadiyya community. I remember many Musleh Maud Day celebrations held at Rabwah during 1949 to 1955 where Hadhrat Maulana Jalal-ud-Din Shams explained this tradition and requested Hadhrat Maulana Abdul-Raheem Dard to keep alive this tradition to come and read the 'Prophetic Announcement.' After his death, I have always tried to maintain this tradition of the 'Dard Family' to read the prophecy at the Musleh Maud Day Meetings. I am most grateful to Mr. Vali Shah, ex Ameer Jamaat U.K. and Mr. Rafiq Ahmad Hayat, Ameer Jamaat of the U.K. Jamaat to allow me to read the Prophecy Of Musleh Maud at the Musleh Maud Day Meeting for the first time after the inauguration of the Bait-ul-Futuh Mosque in February, 2004. I hope that our family members all around the world would keep up this blessed tradition in remembrance of our forefathers and the love of the Promised Messiah and Hadhrat Musleh Maud who started this tradition by selecting Maulana Abdul Raheem Dard to have the unique privilege to keep alive the association of our ancestors with the Promised Messiah. Hadhrat Musleh Maud was a traditionalist and always upheld such tradition in the Ahmadiyya Muslims Jamaat. Hadhrat A.R. Dard and I lived together alone at times at Rabwah from 1949 to 1955. He was the elder brother of my father "Haji" Barkatullah, The First Sub-Post master of Rabwah. My uncle Hadhrat Dard helped and guided me through my under graduate education at Talim-ul-Islam College at Lahore and Rabwah. During my stay with him at Rabwah, he used to narrate many of the incidents of historical importance which were carried out by him under the Divine guidance of Hadhrat Musleh Maud in the fields of politics and religion. I sometimes accompanied him on his travels. Once, he narrated a dream which he had had the night before he was called by the Minister Of India in the British Government to see him in his office in London in 1934. Uncle Dard said, "I saw in my dream that a lion has attacked me. I have obtained a green leafy branch of a tree to defend myself. I beat the Lion with it, slowly, again and again the lion retreats to sit down quietly at the side." He interpreted the dream himself by saying that it was the Divine Guidance from Allah tallah to teach and protect him from the forthcoming attack of the British Government. The Lion is the symbol of Britain. Hadhrat Musleh Maud, Khalifa tul Masih II had directed him to explain the complex situation to the British Government, which had arisen out of the Majlis Ahrar Propagenda Conference at a place in the close vicinity of Qadian. It was a sheer blessing of the prayers of Hadhrat Musleh Maud, The Khalifa, that God Almighty guided him in the dream and showed him the way in which he should explain with dignity and respect, slowly and steadily, to the minister of India the true situation regarding the events in India. He met the minister and accomplished the task very successfully under the divine guidance. Those who work in obedience and according to the instructions of the Khalif a tul Masih, God Almighty Himself becomes their guide and protects them from harm and leads them to success. We see such examples of Allah TaAlla's mercy among the righteous servants of the Khilafat-e-Ahmadiyya today.

When my uncle Dard died many members of our family devoted their lives for Islam and offered themselves to Hadhrat Musleh Maud. I had also offered. In 1959 I was asked by Hadhrat Musleh Maud to resign my post at Sargodha and come to Rabwah. I did so Hadhrat Musleh Maud appointed me as a Naib Nazir (Deputy Secretary) and gave me instructions on how to assist Hadhrat Waliullah Shah Sahib, who was then Nazir Amoor-e-Kharja. Hadhrat Musleh Maud also said that he did not take my uncle Dard with him to Europe this time and he died of this shock. There was a mutual love and complete understanding of purpose between Hadhrat Musleh Maud and Hadhrat Dard. They loved each other for the sake of Islam.

On the 7th December 1955 while Hadhrat Dard was working in the office of Hadhrat Mirza Aziz Ahmad he had the first heart attack at twelve fifteen. Hadhrat Dr. Hashmatullah Khan arrived and administered some medicine. He was carried home and at quarter past two in the afternoon he passed away at Rabwah after serving Islam and Ahmadiyyat for more than half a century. The next day on the 8th December 1955 Hadhrat Musleh Maud led his funeral prayers at the "Paradise Cemetery" where he was buried in the special plot of the companions of the Promised Messiah. On the 9th December, 1955 in his Friday sermon, Hadhrat Musleh Maud, graciously summarized the life and times of Hadhrat Dard and paid glowing tributes to him. Hadhrat Mirza Bashir Ahmad also wrote a lengthy essay with love and affection describing the various talents and qualities of Hadhrat Dard and declared that he belonged to a blessed family which enjoys a special distinction in the history of Ahmadiyyat.

Hadhrat Maulana A.R. Dard has set an example of pioneer service, sacrifice and selfless devotion to the Institution of Khilafat and the Khalifa, which will, Insha'Allah, inspire the future generations of our family to follow his footsteps and others who would come to appreciate his life and devoted services for Islam and Ahmadiyyat.

Matiullah Dard
General Secretary, South East London Ahmadiyya Jamaat

This article was also published in the Ahmadiyya Gazette USA July 2010

Hadhrat Musleh Maud at Quetta in 1948

حضرت خلیفۃ المسیح الثانیؓ کے سفر انگلستان ۱۹۲۴ء کا ایک یادگار فوٹو

بیٹھے ہوئے: ۱۔ حضرت ملک غلام فرید صاحب ۔ حضرت بھائی عبدالرحمٰن صاحب قادیانی ۔
کرسیوں پر: ۱۔ حضرت چوہدری محمد ظفر اللہ خان صاحب ۔ حضرت مولانا عبدالرحیم درد صاحب ۔ حضرت خلیفۃ المسیح الثانیؓ....
حضرت مولانا عبدالرحیم نیر صاحب ۔ حضرت مولانا ذوالفقار علی خان گوہر صاحب ۔
کھڑے ہوئے: ۱۔ حضرت ڈاکٹر حشمت اللہ خان صاحب ۔ حضرت شیخ یعقوب علی عرفانی صاحب ۔ حضرت حافظ روشن علی صاحب
حضرت مولوی محمد الدین صاحب ۔ حضرت مرزا شریف احمد صاحب ۔ محترم عبدالرحمٰن مصری صاحب ۔ حضرت چوہدری فتح محمد صاحب سیال ۔

An Ahmadiyya Muslim 93

Letter

بسم اللہ الرحمٰن الرحیم

Mutteeullah Dard
"PEACE"
4 Goffs Close, Harborne
California Way
Birmingham B32 3XA – UK
Tel. 021 426 5261

15th June, 1999.

میرے پیارے سیدی!
السلام علیکم ورحمۃ اللہ وبرکاتہ

مجھے نہ تو کوئی ایسی دنیاوی منصب حاصل ہے کہ یہ خیال بھی کبھی آتا کہ میری حقیر زندگی کا کچھ ذکر ہیں ہو اور نہ ہی منیں میں طاقت ہے کوئی ایسی زہینیت حاصل ہے کہ یہ ویم کبھی بھی دل و دماغ میں آتا کہ حضور کے اس ادنیٰ ترین غلام کے اپنے کسی عمل کا کوئی ذکر بھی کہیں کرے بلکہ دل ڈرتا رہتا ہے کہ کہیں خدا تعالیٰ اللہ تعالیٰ کی ناراضگی کا موجب نہ بن جائے۔ لیکن نظامِ خلافت کی اطاعت میں اور آپ کے ارشادات کی روشنی میں منفاتی مزدور جماعت احمدیہ کی پرزور ہدایت کے تحت میں نے جماعت احمدیہ کی تاریخ اپنی سوانح عمری کے رنگ میں لکھی ہے جس کا تعلق تاریخی حقائق سے ہے جو قادیان، ڈلہوزی، ربوہ، بی نیوزی لینڈ اور برطانیہ سے متعلق ہیں۔

حضور انور سے نہایت عاجزی سے التجاء ہے اس منسلک مسودہ کو ملاحظہ فرما کر اس کے بارے میں اپنی راہنمائی، مشورہ اور منظوری سے نوازیں تاکہ اسے آپکی خوشنودی اور اجازت سے شائع کرسکوں یا نہ کروں؟

خاکسار
حضور کا ادنیٰ ترین غلام

مطیع اللہ دارد
سیکرٹری تعلیم و تربیت و واقفینِ نو
جماعت احمدیہ برمنگھم

An Ahmadiyya Muslim 94

Letter

VAKALAT-E-TASNEEF

The London Mosque, 16 Gressenhall Road, London SW18 5QL U.K.
Tel: 0181-870-9955 Ext. 416   Tel & Fax: 0181-877-1201

Ref:-   Date:-

Ref. AVT 1834/09.04.2000
Mr. Muteeullah Dard
"Peace"
4 Goffs Close
California Way
Harborne Rise
Birmingham B32 3XA

Re. An Ahmadiyya Muslim Autobiography

Dear Mr. Dard,
Assalamo Alaikum Wa Rehmatullahe Wa Barakatohu

Further to my letter to you of March 06, 2000, it is to inform you that according to the instructions of Hadhrat Khalifatul Masih IV, the manuscript is being sent to Rabwah for further checking and report. I shall be informing you about the decision regarding permission of publishing your book after receiving report from Rabwah.

Wassalam.
Yours sincerely,

MUNIR-UD-DIN SHAMS
Addl. Vakil-ut-Tasneef

Islamabad, Sheephatch Lane, Tilford Surrey GU10 2AQ U.K.   Fax: 01252-783148

Letter

VAKALAT-E-TASNEEF

The London Mosque, 16 Gressenhall Road, London SW18 5QL U.K.
Tel: 0181-870-9955 Ext. 416   Tel & Fax: 0181-877-1201

Ref:- AVT—1911   Date:- 18-8-2000

مکرمی ڈاکٹر امیر صاحب یو کے

السلام علیکم ورحمۃ اللہ وبرکاتہ

آپ نے مکرم مطیع الرحمٰن درد صاحب آف برمنگھم کی کتاب
An Ahmadiyya Muslim Auto Biography بغرض حصول منظوری عنایات
فرمائی تھی۔

مکرم مطیع الرحمٰن صاحب کو اپنے طور پر اسے شائع کرنے اور تقسیم/فروخت
کرنے کی اجازت دی جاتی ہے۔ براہ کرم انہیں مطلع فرما دیں۔
مسودہ بھی آپ کو ساتھ مرسل ہے۔

والسلام
خاکسار
منیر الدین شمس
ایڈیشنل وکیل التصنیف

نوٹ (۱/۲)
بغرض اطلاع مطیع اللہ درد
دارالعلوم لاہور
امضاء
امیر کے لئے
19.8.2000

An Ahmadiyya Muslim   96

Certificate

Lautoka Muslim High School

Founded in 1957 by Fiji Muslim League

Principal: Mr. K.S. Reddy
Phone No. 176

Secretary: Board of Governors
Mr. Imam Ali
Phone No. 180

P.O. Box No. 119
LAUTOKA, FIJI

TO WHOM IT MAY CONCERN

It affords me pleasure to write this reference in respect of Mr. Mutiullah Dard, M.A., who has served as a lecturer of English Literature and also served in the capacity of Career Advisor and Cashier at this High School for three years (1961-1963).

The departure of Mr. Dard is a great loss to the colony generally and an irrepairable set-back to this Institution in particular. For sometime to come, the Institution may not see another such a talented, cultured and exceedingly popular teacher as Mr. Dard—a person of integrity.

It is a pleasure in recommending this gentleman to those who may require the services of a competent, intelligent and thoroughly honest person to a position of trust.

May God spare him to serve mankind.

20th September, 1963.

K.S. Reddy
PRINCIPAL

****

Certificate

Wilkes Green Junior School,
Antrobus Road,
Handsworth,
Birmingham, 21 9N. T.
February 23rd. 1971

To Whom It May Concern:

 Mr. M. Dard joined the Staff of this school in April 1970. He came here on promotion having been the successful candidate interviewed for the Scale 1 Post for Immigrant Welfare.

 Since then Mr. Dard has dealt with any problems among the children or parents when there has been a language problem. When necessary he has visited the homes of the children. During the last Summer Holiday he helped to organise a four weeks' English course at this school for parents who could not speak English.

 Mr. Dard had a third year class for one term and since September he has been in charge of a 4th. year class. The children have been well taught and well prepared for the Junior School Leaving Examination. There is a pleasant teaching atmosphere in his classroom and the children are very well controlled.

 Art and Mathematics are a special interest of Mr. Dard and this is evident in the work of his children. Not only is the children's work displayed in his classroom but it is also attractively displayed in the school corridors and entrance hall.

 With his class Mr. Dard has taken the occasional morning assembly and he now preparing a special Easter Service.

 Mr. Dard volunteered to take charge of the school chess team. He has given his own time to train them in the dinner hour and to take them to matches after school.

 Mr. Dard is highly regarded by the children and their parents. He is ready for further promotion and I am confident he will make a capable Deputy Head Teacher.

I. Jones. (Mr)
Headmaster.

Certificate

CITY OF BIRMINGHAM EDUCATION COMMITTEE
AUDLEY JUNIOR SCHOOL

Headmaster:
Mr. A. M. GIBBS
Telephone:
021-783 3139

AUDLEY ROAD,
STECHFORD,
BIRMINGHAM 33.
16th January 1970.

Mr. Matiullah Dard has been on this staff since September 1966, and has taken classes 2.2, 3.2 and 4.1. He has shown himself to be a competent teacher, with good class control, a firm disciplinarian without the heavy hand, and has accomodated himself well to the demands made by the newer methods and the many facilities in this school. He has been a willing helper in many school activities outside his classroom, House Meetings, Sports Days, chess practice, school functions, exhibitions, outings, etc.

He is keen to continue his higher studies and has applied to go on several courses.

With the staff he has always been a pleasing personality, with a ready sense of humour, helpful and accomodating to all.

I am sure he will be most conscientious and persevering in any newer or higher posts he achieves.

A.M. Gibbs

Certificate

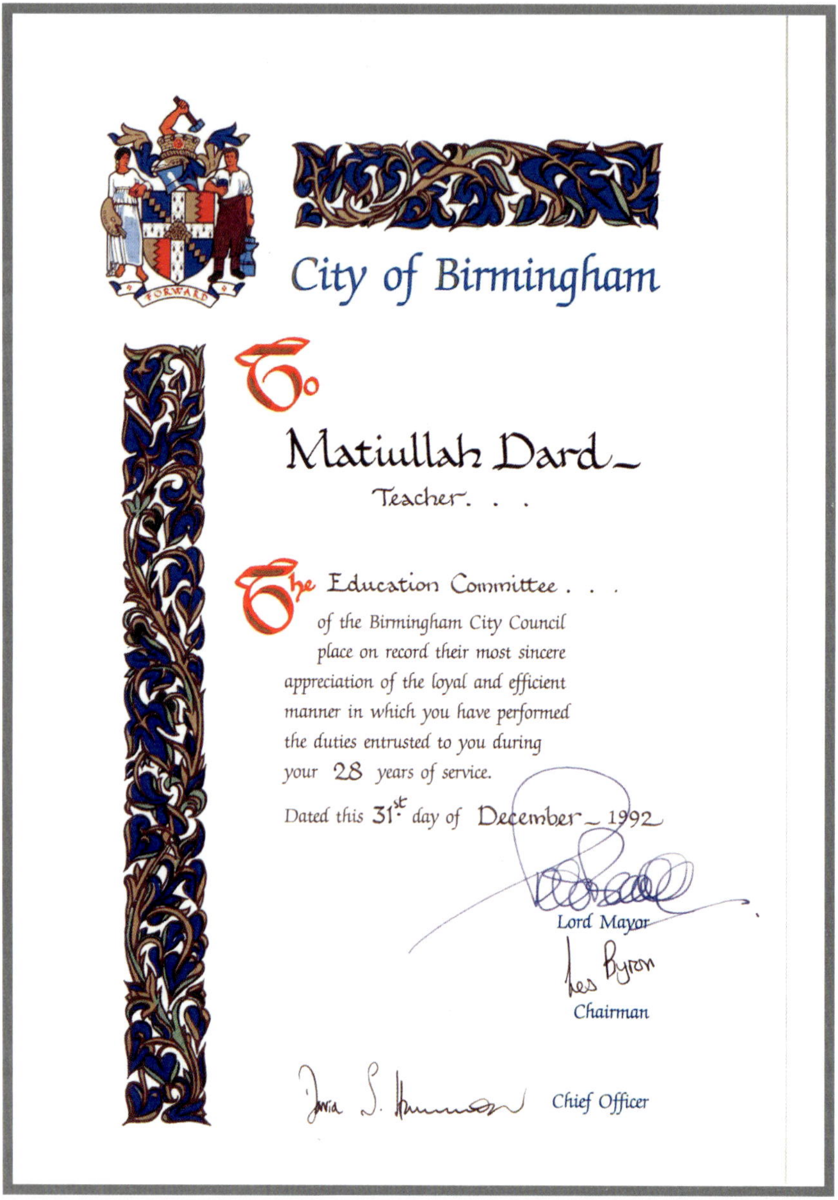

City of Birmingham

To

Matiullah Dard

Teacher . . .

The Education Committee . . . of the Birmingham City Council place on record their most sincere appreciation of the loyal and efficient manner in which you have performed the duties entrusted to you during your 28 years of service.

Dated this 31st day of December 1992

Lord Mayor

Les Byron
Chairman

Chief Officer

News Paper

EVENING MAIL, THURSDAY, AUGUST 24, 2000

Urdu pioneer to leave city

Groundbreaking teacher retires

By Zoe Chamberlain

THE man who introduced Urdu into Birmingham schools is leaving the city after nearly 40 years of teaching, it was revealed today.

Matiullah Dard was one of the first Asian teachers in the city and also helped to break down the barriers for Asian councillors.

Now the 64-year-old is selling his Harborne home to live with his son in Belgium after retiring early due to ill health.

Develop skills

The Pakistani, who was also on the board of Birmingham's Community Health Council, said: "At first Urdu was only available at break, lunchtimes and on Saturdays. I thought it was important for Asian children to develop skills in their own language as well as in English.

"The majority of children who choose to learn Urdu are of Pakistani origin but born here. Learning their native language helps them to realise the value of their culture and heritage."

Mr Dard became the city council's community linguist liaison officer and visited schools throughout Birmingham as well as pupil's homes to check on communication difficulties.

"Sometimes parents did not ask their children what they had been doing at school and how they were getting on," he said.

"I tried to encourage them to take an active interest as this helps their children to develop at school."

After arriving in Birmingham in 1964, Mr Dard taught at Audley School, in Stechford, Clifton Junior and Infants, in Balsall Heath, and Park View, in Alum Rock.

In Handsworth, he worked at Wilkes Green Junior School, Grove Junior School and Rookery Road Junior School.

He then went on to run the Urdu department at Joseph Chamberlain College where he retired in April 1999.

"I was told I could have become a head teacher, but I enjoyed my pioneering work and felt I would be more beneficial to people if I kept pushing for Urdu development.

"There is talk of setting up ethnic minority schools in some of the inner city areas of Birmingham. I think it's much better for everyone to be integrated and to learn moral and ethical issues rather than religious beliefs.

"I shall be sad to leave Birmingham because it's been a major part of my life. I'm proud I did my bit."

zoe_chamberlain@mrn.co.uk

■ MATIULLAH DARD: Moving to Belgium to be with his son.
Picture: Steve Murphy

An Ahmadiyya Muslim

News Paper

Scholar follows in footsteps of pioneer uncle

Mosque crusade a family tradition

By Lisa Smith

A BIRMINGHAM scholar is to re-open a dilapidated city school as a mosque and follow in the footsteps of his uncle who opened Britain's first mosque 76 years ago.

Matiullah Dard and fellow members of the Ahmadiyya Muslims have taken over the old Tilton Road school in Bordesley Green and have now spent almost half a million pounds of their own funds transforming it.

The new mosque will eventually be the biggest in the area in terms of what it covers and will feature rooms for prayer, education and community facilities such as sports for local youngsters.

President

The official opening in a few weeks time will also make history for Matiullah who was the region's first elected president of the Ahmadiyya Muslims.

In 1924 his uncle Hazrat Chaudhary Fateh Rahim Dard opened the first Islamic mosque in Britain in in Putney, London.

But modern-day Ahmadis claim they have had a difficult time since they were denounced by the Pakistani government who accused them of being non-Muslim and many members are now persecuted in their home country.

Mr Dard said: "We are very excited about our new mosque which will be a wonderful facility for local people and converting was actually built in 1889 the same year our movement started."

He said the Ahmadiyya Muslims were peace-loving and their beliefs were almost parallel to those of early Christians.

■ BIG PLANS: Matiullah Dard at the Tilton Road School site

Ahmadiyyah Muslims in particular. "It is ironic that I should follow my uncle who opened the first Islamic mosque in Britain and it is also a coincidence that the old school we have been

■ HAZRAT DARD

lisa_smith@xxx.co.uk

News Paper

MILLENNIBRUM

EVENING MAIL, MONDAY DECEMBER 4, 2000

Missionary sewed the seeds in the UK

MATIULLAH Dard has an association with England that goes back to 1913 when his first uncle, Hadhrat Choudhary F M Sayyal came as the first Muslim Ahmadiyya Missionary to England. Another uncle came in 1924 to attend an important religious conference and accompany the Calif as his secretary.

They were instrumental in building the first mosque in England, in Putney. Ahmadiyya Muslim Association was a new movement started by Hadhrat Mirza Ghulam Ahmad in 1889 and now has more than 80 million members worldwide.

Matiullah says "I was a founder member of the Ahmadiyya Muslim Association in Birmingham 36 years ago and established an advice bureau where people could come and seek advice.

"The city has given us the listed building of the old Tilton Road School in Bordesley Green and it has become a mosque and community centre. We've tried to infuse the spirit of tolerance and understanding."

EVENING MAIL, THURSDAY, NOVEMBER 9, 2000

Bid to build largest mosque

By Lisa Smith

A MUSLIM community which built Britain's first ever mosque is pressing ahead with work to create the largest mosque in Birmingham.

The Dar-ul-Barakat mosque is being created in the Victorian former Tilton Road school, in Bordesley Green, and although the outer shell is now complete it is expected to be at least a year before it can be officially opened.

The mosque is being created by members of the Ahmadiyya Muslim Association, a group formed in Birmingham 36 years ago. They have faced persecution ever since 1984 when leader Mirza Tahir Ahmad was denounced by General Zia and the government of Pakistan. The association now has more than 80 million members in 170 countries throughout the world and is still a pioneer in building mosques throughout Europe.

Matiullah Dard, who helped to found the movement in Birmingham and was elected first president of the group in the city, said: "Our association are working hard to convert the old school back to its Victorian splendour. It is as though this building was meant for us – the school was founded in 1889, the year our movement started".

People wanting to find our more about the religion are invited to contact the mosque at 85 Tilton Road or contact Mr Dard on 426 5261.

■ MATIULLAH DARD

An Ahmadiyya Muslim 103

News Paper

16 Wednesday, December 10, 2003
The Mercury
icsouthlondon.co.uk
News

Muslim's message of tolerance

HIS uncle set up the first UK mosque in 1926. Now Matiullah Dard tells KEELY SHERBIRD about the dream of seeing a 'beautiful mosque' for South-east London

MATIULLAH DARD, 69, moved south to Thamesmead six months ago after a long career as a Birmingham teacher.

He is one of 215 million worldwide members of the Ahmadiyya branch of Islam, which was established in 1889.

Ahmadis believe the founder of their community was a prophet who, in Mr Dard's words, came to "clean the beautiful picture of Islam and remove the dirt and dust which the passage of time has put on it".

The Ahmadis' motto is "love for all, hatred for none".

The first mosque in the UK - the London Mosque in Putney - was becoming overcrowded so the Ahmadiyya Muslim Community built one of the largest mosques in Europe in Morden.

It is called the Baitul Futuh Mosque, cost around £5million and opened in May.

Now Mr Dard would like to expand his community's work into South-east London. He said: "We are the pioneers of building mosques, schools and helping humanity. The [South-east London Ahmadiyya Muslims] community area covers Lewisham, Dartford, Bromley - a wide area. Some of us can't go to Morden or the London Mosque. Previously we had a house in Lewisham opposite Goldsmiths College but not any more. To begin with we need a mission house and then we need to find a place to build a beautiful mosque."

Mr Dard's connection with South-east London began 40 years ago.

He said: "The first night I spent in this country, November 9, 1963, was in a dentist friend's house in Powis Street [Woolwich]. They were Hindus, but as Ahmadi Muslims we not only believe in tolerance and respect for other religions we practise that as well and can also name our children after their prophets."

Born in India, Mr Dard moved to Pakistan when he was 12 and stayed there for another 12 years. He moved again to be one of the co-founders of the Ahmadiyya community in Fiji. Once in Birmingham he worked as a primary school teacher and ended his teaching career as a head of department at a sixth-form college.

He also worked for the community health council and took an active role in promoting Urdu.

Mr Dard, who has one son who lives in the US, is the foreign affairs secretary of the South-east London community.

Matiullah Dard (left) with Hadhrat Mirza Masroor Ahmad, head of the Ahmadiyya Muslim Community and fifth successor of the founder of the community, who gave the inaugural address at the Baitul Futuh Mosque, Morden

An Ahmadiyya Muslim   104

News Paper

The Mercury

mercury-today.co.uk

The Mercury, Wednesday, August 19, 2009

News

COUNTRY'S FOUNDER PERSUADED TO RETURN TO POLITICS BY LONDON IMAM

'Pakistan exists thanks to uncle'

By JULIA LEWIS

THE uncle of a Thamesmead man could be said to have been indirectly responsible for the creation of Pakistan.

August 14, Pakistan Independence Day, is a date of great significance for Pakistanis everywhere but it has a particular resonance for Mattullah Dard, of Hill View Drive.

Mattullah Dard is vice-chairman of Bexley Multi-Faith Forum and Thamesmead Inter-Faith Forum.

It was Mr Dard's uncle, Maulana Abdur Rahmin Dard, who persuaded Mohammed Ali Jinnah, the founder and first leader of Pakistan, to leave London to go back home to India.

Jinnah, himself a Muslim, had been involved in politics in India and was particularly concerned about the situation of Muslims in the predominantly Hindu country.

In the early 1930s, having despaired of any progress being made in getting the two communities to live together peacefully, he left India and worked as a barrister in London.

At the time, Mr Dard's uncle, who died in 1955, was Imam at the London Mosque in Southfields and he had been instructed by the spiritual leader of the Ahmadiyya Muslims, Hadhrat Khalifatul Masih II, to persuade Jinnah to return home to take part in politics again.

Imam Dard and Jinnah became good friends and met regularly to talk about the situation in India but it was difficult to convince him.

Mr Dard, 74, said: "Jinnah was a very stern man. Even Lord Mountbatten said he was a difficult man to deal with.

"He was really obstinate. He did not change his mind easily.

"My uncle told me about the whole incident. He said he asked Mr Jinnah many times why he was living in London and why he quit politics."

Then one day the Imam made a remark that finally hit home with the politician.

Mr Dard said: "My uncle suggested that if he did not go back to India he would be a traitor to the Muslim cause. That affected him very much.

"He was stunned and remained silent for a while. Then he asked my uncle what he should do.

"Mr Jinnah respected my uncle very much."

In a speech he subsequently made at the London Mosque, Jinnah acknowledged the Imam's role in his decision to return to political life, saying: "The eloquent persuasion of the Imam left me no escape."

Jinnah returned to India in 1934 and became Governor General of Pakistan when it became an independent state on August 14, 1947.

Mr Dard said: "I am very happy and proud that I am related to the man who sent Jinnah back to make something of Pakistan.

"If he had not gone back, there would have been no Pakistan."

Mattullah Dard and, inset left, Maulana Abdur Rahmin Dard

An Ahmadiyya Muslim   105

Friendly Observation

بِسْمِ اللهِ الرَّحْمٰنِ الرَّحِيْمِ
Bismillah ar-Rahman ar-Rahim

NAHMADOHOO WA NOSALLY ALA RASOOLEHIL KAREEM WA ALA ABDEHIL MASSIHIL MAOOD WA ALA KHULFA'E HIM AJMAEEN

FIFTY YEARS OF MY ASSOCIATION WITH MATIULLAH DARD: A GLANCE

I am grateful to my Creator for guiding me to the Light of Truth at very young age from the ocean of darkness all around me. Along the way, I had the good fortune to know my friend, Matiullah Dard, during those wonderful days of 1955 in Lahore, (a most beautiful city in Pakistan at that time). In all humility, I am happy to add a few lines to his upcoming eventful biography about our historical journeys, together and separate, on the winding and merging paths of our lives.

I joined Ahmadiyya Family of the Promised Messiah alaihisslam in early 1953 against the wishes of my father. As a consequence, I was cut off from my ancient family. I relished the honour to be introduced to many divines in Ahmadiyya Community, including Hazrat Maulana Abdur Raheem Dard. I remember meeting Matiullah Dard sometimes during 1955 (after we had both joined the Punjab University's Master of Psychology program through Islamia College Lahore, Pakistan.) At that time, he did not know that I was a True Moslim too!

Soon, he transferred to Government College, Lahore. This was very upsetting for our Professor, Dr. Saeedullah, Head of Psychology Department at Islamia College. Still, Dr. Saeedullah would welcome Matiullah and love to talk to him, in pure Punjabi language of course, whenever he came to visit our department. He always looked very enthusiastic and was quite popular among his peers and professors.

Later, I learnt from Matiullah that Dr. Saeedullah had told him that he went to Qadian along with Dr. Sir Muhammad Iqbal and Saifuddeen Kitchloo for Bai'at at the hands of Hazrat Massih Maood alaihisslam. Dr. Saeedullah was said to be also a regular subscriber to Al-Fazl newspaper. However, they apparently all got separated from Ahmadiyyat for some political reasons of their own.

After completing the **Master in Psychology** degree, I learnt that Matiullah had gone to Australia for Missionary work while I **wasted** some precious years trying in vain to change the corrupt political climate in Pakistan. (I wish I **should have** spent all that time in the company of Hazrat Musleh Maood, RA) We both were joined in **London in 1964**. He began his new career at Birmingham (as is beautifully illustrated in this volume) while I worked as a Psychologist in Essex, London Borough of Redbridge and Sussex. In England, we had many common friends, including Imam Basheer Ahmad Rafiq, Sir Muhammad Zaffarullah Khan and Professor Abdus Salam. I came to America in 1976, nearly two hundred years late!

It was a pleasant surprise for me to discover in 2002 that a new and wonderful family coming from Holland to Research Triangle Jama'at was my own family, family of my dear friend and brother, Matiullah Dard. I pray that our families will also keep this affinity in the future generations to serve humanity together under the guidance of Khilafate Ahmadiyya in True Islam. Ameen.

An ordinary & humble servant of God Almighty in True Islam,
Dr. Rasheed Sayyed Azam,
Apex, North Carolina, USA.   November 2002.

An Ahmadiyya Muslim   106

Friendly Observation

A MEMOIR

It is a pleasure to find Matiullah Dard, a member of the Dard Family, in our midst here in Research Triangle, North Carolina, USA, and share memories of early childhood days with him spent in Mohalla Darul Anwar, Qadian. We have much to share between us in so far as memories of those early days are concerned. The rest that we could not share he has dexterously put in the form of his personal memoir. He appears to have special knack in preserving personal account of his life with documentary evidences and photographs. That makes the description very convincing. His academic background, his stay close to the dignitaries of the Jamaat in Rabwah and wherever he moved during the course of his subsequent life, at Fiji islands, New Zealand, Australia and then settling down in Birmingham (England) etc. has been very nicely and crisply depicted in his memoir. His personal account is, therefore, in no way a personal account of his life but a Jamaat history. It tells about the activities of the young and old of the Jamaat, including himself, which they render in the service of the Jamaat. He has been personal witness to many historic events of the Jamaat. In recounting them he re-enlivens many Jamaat "Bazurgs" who are now precious part of the history. In reading Matiullah Dard's narrative we, his age mate, can vividly bring into our mind those valuable personages. As far as his personal merits are concerned he appears to have inherited love and sincerity for the Jamaat from his immediate ancestors and has remained devoted to the service of the Jamaat wherever he went throughout his life. This is not only commendable but enviable also. As far as his skill in rendering this history in black and white his expression is excellent, crisp and precise. It is a pleasure to read him.

HAMEED-UL-MAHAMID MA
111 Summerglow Ct.
Cary, NC 27513 USA

November 23, 2002

Glimpses of my life

At Baitul Futuh Mosque on the occasion of Eid ul Fitr 2009

Wtih Hadhrat Khalifatul Masih V (atba) 2003

Wtih Hadhrat Khalifatul Masih V (atba) 2004

An Ahmadiyya Muslim 109

Wtih Hadhrat Khalifatul Masih IV (rh) 1999

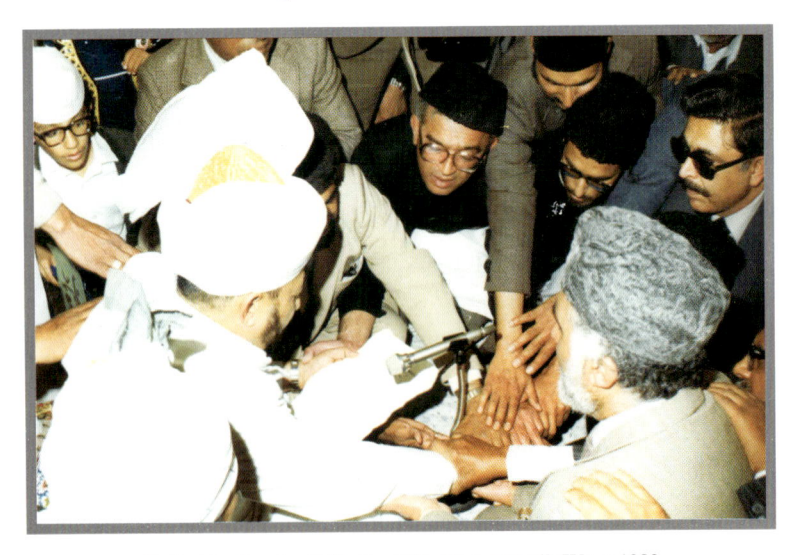

Bait at the hands of Hadhrat Khalifatul Masih IV (rh) 1983

An Ahmadiyya Muslim 110

M. D. Shams, M. U. Dard, Nawabzada S. A. Pasha, B. A. Rafiq (Imam) &
A. W. Adam Chugtai with Hadhrat Khalifatul Masih III (rh) 1967 at The London Mosque

Hadhrat Khalifatul Masih IV (rh) at Birmingham 1984

Matiullah Dard with Sahibzada M. M. Ahmed at Ahmed Salam's Wedding London

Matiullah Dard with Hadhrat Sahibzada Mirza Mansoor Ahmed at Dar ul Barakat, Birmingham

Hadhrat Mirza Nasir Ahmad III (rh) in London in 1967

Matiullah Dard with Professor Abdul Salam at his son's marriage

**Fourth Nasir Tarbiyyati Class at Mehmood Hall London,
24th December 1982 to 1st, January 1983**

An Ahmadiyya Muslim 114

Sahibzada Mirza Anas Ahmed & Matiullah Dard

Maulana Bashir Ahmad Orchid & Matiullah Dard at Oxford Mission House

Matiullah Dard on Italian Ship TV Roma, Flota Laura enroute to Italy

Matiullah Dard & Dr. Vijay Mohan Bhatnagar in Cairo, Egypt 963

Nurud din Latif, Jalal Latif, Matiullah Dard, Rasheed Azam & Hameed ul Mahamid in North Carolina USA

Matiullah Dard, Master Ahmed Krishan Dard, & Abdul Rashid Hyderabadi at Birmingham 1965

Matiullah Dard & Fijian High Commissioner for UK in London 1974

Hanif Ibraheem Dard (my nephew) & Matiullah Dard at Rawalpindi 2003

An Ahmadiyya Muslim

Asmatullah & Matiullah Dard at Canberra Australia 1963

Matiullah Dard at the
University of Auckland, New Zealand 1963

Matiullah Dard at a Park in
Auckland, New Zealand 1963

First Bait of the 2nd Century, Islamabad, Surrey, U.K. 24th March 1989

Matiullah Dard (Ravian) at Govt. College Lahore 1957

Matiullah Dard & Harbhajan Singh at Ahmaidyya Muslim Convention 2009

An Ahmadiyya Muslim 119

Alfazl Excerpt

Alfazl Excerpt

Alfazl Excerpt

روزنامہ الفضل 21 جون 2010ء

تاریخ احمدیت برطانیہ کا ایک روشن ورق

عیسائی پادری ڈاکٹر بلی گراہم کا روحانی مقابلہ سے فرار

مکرم مطیع اللہ دردر صاحب

امریکہ کے مشہور عیسائی مناد ڈاکٹر بلی گراہم کو عیسائی دنیا میں کافی شہرت حاصل ہوئی اور وہ اپنی زندگی میں مختلف ممالک میں جا کر عیسائیت کی منادی کرتے رہے۔ حقیقت کے اس مناد کو صرف جماعت احمدیہ کے افراد نے للکارا اور حضرت مسیح موعود کے دعاؤں کی بنیاد پر ہر بار ان کو شکست دی جا چکی ہے۔ سب سے پہلے افریقہ کے ملکوں میں محترم مولانا شیخ مبارک احمد صاحب مربی سلسلہ نے 3 مارچ 1961 کو ڈاکٹر بلی گراہم کے نام ایک خط بھیجا جس میں ان کے سامنے انجیل کے اصولوں پر روبرو عالاج دین حق اور عیسائیت کی تحریر کرنے کا طریق کار رکھا اور دعوت مباہلہ کی۔ جس کا تذکرہ خود حضرت مسیح موعودؑ نے دعا بر مہتم BBC Midland Radio پر اور ایک دوسرے کمرشل ریڈیو BRMB پر اس شیخ کا خوب چرچا ہوا کئی بار خبروں میں اسے نشر کیا گیا۔ BRMB ریڈیو پر خاکسار کا بس منٹ کا انٹرویو نشر ہوا جس میں احمدیت کی دعوت کا بہترین موقع اللہ تعالیٰ نے مجھے اپنے فضل سے عطایا۔ جب ہزاروں لوگوں نے سنا اور چھڑوں کے بعد مجھے ڈاکٹر بلی گراہم کے ڈائریکٹر کی طرف سے وہی جواب دہرایا گیا جو انہوں نے افریقہ میں دیا تھا۔ لیکن اس بار جواب میں لکھا کہ وہ دعا کے ذریعہ سے مریضوں کی صحت یاب ہونے کا تسلیم کرتے ہیں مگر اس وقت دوبارہ سارا وقت صرف انگلینڈ میں تبلیغ کرنے میں گزارا چاہتے ہیں۔ اس لیے اس تبلیغ کو قبول کرنے سے معذور ہیں اور انکار کرکے راہِ فرار اختیاری کی۔ اس تبلیغ کی تفصیلی رپورٹ Review of Religions کے شمارہ دسمبر 1984ء میں شائع ہو چکی ہے۔

صاحب بر عظیم آ کے ان تو وان کہ حضرت مسیح موعود والا دعا کا شیخ جو لاعلاج مریضوں کی شفا پانے کے لئے تھا اور آپ نے انہیں جماعت کی طرف سے تبلیغ کرنے کی وہ تجویز دعا کے ذریعے چھ غیب اللہ تعالیٰ کا شہود ہے وی۔ ان تحقیقات اور ناطل و فرق مباہلہ ہوسکیائی ظاہر ہوجا۔ حضور اقدس نے اس حقیر کو ایک خادم احمدیت کو اجازت عنایت فرمائی اور خاکسار نے ایک انگریزی رجسٹرڈ خط کے ذریعہ ڈاکٹر بلی گراہم کو مباہلہ دعا کا تبلیغ دیا۔

ڈاکٹر بلی گراہم نے جواب دیا "میرا کام مجھے دعوت دے کہ میں مریضوں کو چکا کرنا نہیں" عیسائی حلقوں کی طرف سے ڈاکٹر بلی گراہم کو مجبور کیا جانے لگا کہ وہ تبلیغ قبول کرکے عیسائیت کی سچائی کا شہود دیں ورنہ عیسائیت کو بہت زک پہنچے گی کہ وہ آدمی جو یکتا یکتا ہو اے وہ بھی افریقہ کے غیر از جماعت نے 1984ء دسمبر Review of Religions کے شمارہ میں شائع ہو چکا ہے۔

مکرم شیخ مبارک احمد صاحب کو مبارک باد دی اور اقرار کیا کہ آپ نے عیسائیت کے بالمقابل دین حق کا جھنڈا خوب بلند رکھا"۔ اسی طرح ڈاکٹر بلی گراہم افریقہ میں جہاں بھی گئے احمدی مربیوں نے ان کا پورا پورا تعاقب کیا۔ مکرم قیم صاحب تم سیپی مشتری انچارج مغربی افریقہ نے لیگوس میں بلی گراہم کو مباہلہ دعا دیا گر وہ اس منظرہ کرنے کی جرات نہ کر سکے۔

(تاریخ احمدیت جلد ہیجدہم صفحہ 288-289)

1984ء میں ڈاکٹر بلی گراہم نے "مشن انگلینڈ" کا اعلان کرکے برطانیہ کے شہروں میں تبلیغ شروع کی تو خاکسار نے حضرت مرزا طاہر احمد خلیفۃ المسیح الرابعؒ کی خدمت میں بحیثیت سیکرٹری دعوت الی اللہ جماعت احمدیہ برعظیم اجازت کی درخواست کی جب بلی گراہم

ڈاکٹر بلی گراہم کے افریقہ اور انگلستان میں احمدی مربیان کے دیے گئے تبلیغ سے فرار دین حق کی سچائی کا ایک بین ثبوت ہے اور حضرت مسیح موعود کی صداقت پر مہر تصدیق ہے۔

امریکہ میں ڈاکٹر ڈوئی اور ہندوستان میں پنڈت لکھرام اور عبداللہ آتم کی دعا کا آغاز تاریخ احمدیت کا وہ سنہری باب ہیں اور ہمارا نظام خلافت کی برکت سے شاید آخری سیخ تک دین حق کی راہنمائی کی میری روح پر ورپلکتاں ہے۔ دین حق کی صداقت میں ہمارا زندہ اللہ تعالیٰ ہمیشہ دکھاتا رہے گا۔ تا ہمیشہ دین حق تمام دوسرے ادیان پر قرآن مجید کی آیت کے مطابق غالب آ جائے۔

An Ahmadiyya Muslim   122

A Letter from Maulana Dost Mohammad Shahid
"Historian of Ahmadiyyat"

بسم الله الرحمن الرحیم

Department of the History of Ahmadiyyat
(KHALAFAT LIBRARY)

Ref. No. _____   RABWAH (Pakistan).   Dated 26 APR 2000

معظم و مکرم جناب مطیع الله درد صاحب

السلام علیکم ورحمۃ اللہ وبرکاتہ

آنکدرم کا بیش قیمت یادداشتیں "AN AHMADI LIFE" کے زیرعنوان موصول ہوگئیں اور آپ کے لیے بہت بہت دعائیں نکلیں رب کریم آپ کو بیش ازبیش خدمات جلیلہ کی سعادت بخشے اور مرکزوں سے مسرور لمحہ فعال زندگی سے نوازے۔ آمین

یادداشتوں کو شائع و ریکارڈ کر لیا گیا ہے اور ان شاء اللہ ان سے تدوینِ تاریخِ احمدیت کے سلسلہ میں حتی الوسع بہر طور بہرہ استفادہ کیا جائے گا۔ فجزاکم اللہ و نیز اس لطف کی اشدی حد زیادہ سے زیادہ دوبارہ شکریہ

والسلام
دوست محمد شاہد
مورخ احمدیت

Matiullah Dard

Mob: 079 8527 2063   Email: matiullahdard@hotmail.com

Personal Information
Date of Birth: 9/9/1934
Place of Birth: Qadian, India
Nationality: British
Sex: Male

Moosi
Wasiyyat No: 78091

Education

1973-1974   **University of Birmingham**
PhD. Research Scholar Theology

1955-1958   **University of Punjab**
MA Psychology: Second Class
DES London; Qualified Teacher No. R.P. 64/2102

1951-1955   **University of Punjab**
BA English, Philosophy, Urdu and Islamiyyat: Pass

Experience

1959-1960   **Deputy Director (Naib Nazar) Central Ahmadiyya Muslim Organisation Rabwah, Pakistan**

1958-1959   **Public Relations and Social Education Officer, Government of Pakistan**

Teaching Experience

7th July 1993-2nd February 1999
Lecturer - Linguist and Head of Department, Joseph Chamberlain Sixth Form College, Birmingham

1st January 1987-31st December 1992
Linguist Advisory Lecturer/ ESL-EFL, Joseph Chamberlain Sixth Form College, Birmingham
Scale D Post Holder

1st September 1984-31st August 1987
Teacher of Urdu/Punjabi and Liason Linguist between community languages and modern European languages, Consortium Languages Team, City of Birmingham Education Department
Scale 4 Post Holder

1st September 1983-31st August 1984
On the Peripatetic Teachers Team of Community Languages Unit for Secondary Schools, City of Birmingham
Scale 3 Post Holder

1st September 1974-31st August 1983
Home/School Liaison Teacher, Clifton Junior and Infant Schools, Balsall Heath, Birmingham
Scale 3 Post Holder

1st January 1973-31st August 1974
On the Mobile Supply Teachers Force for Primary Schools, Various Schools, City of Birmingham
Scale 2 Post Holder

1st May 1970-31st December 1970
Post of Responsibility for Immigrant Welfare, Wilkes Green Junior School, Handsworth, Birmingham

1st September 1966-30th April 1970
Audley Junior School, Stechford, Birmingham

6th April 1964-31st August 1966
Upper Thomas St. Junior School, Aston, Birmingham

1st January 1961-30th September 1963
Lecturer in English Language and Literature, Lautoka Muslim High School, Lautoka, Fiji

Interests

Sports, Reading, Music, Cooking and Travelling. Visited Australia, Belgium, Germany, New Zealand, Italy, France, Fiji Islands and U S A.

Responsibilities: Social Welfare, Voluntary Work

1. President: Ahmadiyya Muslim Community Birmingham 1967 to 1975.

2. Member of the following;
   a. Junior Sub-Group, SHAP Working Party on World Religions in Education, 1971-1974
   b. City of Birmingham Community Relations Council, 1972 to 1975
   c. East Birmingham Community Health Council, 1975 to 1981
   d. Executive Committee of the East Birmingham Community Health Council, 1975 to 1983
   e. Malvern St. Play-Centre Management Committee, Balsall Heath, Birmingham, 1975 to 1983
   f. Balsall Heath Carnival Committee Birmingham, 1977 to 1983

3. Manager: Teacher Representative. The Governing Body for Clifton Junior and Infant Schools, 1980 to 1982.

4. Vice-Chairman: The Governing Body for Clifton Junior and Infant Schools, 1980 to1982

5. Chairman: Urdu Language Panel, Multi-Cultural Resource Unit, Birmingham L.E.A, 1980 to 1986.

6. Vice-Chairman: Birmingham Home/School Liaison Teacher's Association, 1982 to 1983.

7. Moderator and Trainer of Teachers for Urdu. GCSE-MEG 1986 to 1988.

8. Chief Examiner: West Midlands Examining Board-Mode 3 CSE 1985 to 1987.

9. Moderator/Examiner for Urdu Midland Examining Group 1989 to 1993.

10. Chairman: Syllabus of English Committee, Jamia Ahmadiyya International, U.K., 2000 to 2001.

11. Secretary Foreign Affairs, South East London Ahmadiyya Muslim Association, 2003 2010.

12. Secretary-General, South East London Ahmadiyya Muslim Association, 2004-2010.

13. Vice-Chairman, Bexley Multi Faith Forum and Thamesmead Interfaith Forum, London, 2008- . . . .

14. Vice President and Talim & Tarbiyyat Secretary, Bexley & Greenwich Ahmadiyya Muslim Jamaat, 1st, July 2010 - . . . .

Talim-ul-Islam College, Lahore
Character Certificate

Name* MATIULLAH DARD Father's Name* Haji Barkatullah
Home Address* 4. Mcleod Road, Lahore.
Date of birth† 9. 9. 1935
Joined here May 1951   Left here April. 1955

Academic Record:

Year	Roll No.	Marks	Division	Institution
Matric. 1951	2357	453	2nd	PRIVATE (JHANG District)

Subjects/Distinction English, History, Geography, Science, Mathematics, Drawing, Urdu.

Year	Roll No.	Marks	Division	Institution
F.A./F.Sc. 1953	8032		3rd	T.I. College, Lahore

Subjects: 1. English, 2. History 3. Philosophy, Persian Optional Islamiyat
Distinction

Year	Roll No.	Marks	Division	Institution
B.A./B.Sc./Hons 1955	4154	209	3rd	T.I. College Rabwah

Subjects: 1. English, 2. Philosophy 3. Urdu Optional Islamiyyat Hons. x
Distinctions   Roll of Honour

Year	Roll No.	Marks	Division	Institution
M.A./M.Sc. 1958	415	315	2nd	Later Govt. College (Lahore) student

Subject Psychology Distinctions   Roll of Honour

Sports/Games/U.O.T.C., etc., member U.O.T.C.
Member or Captain first team member hockey XI Prizes first prizes in debates
College Colours   University Blue
Other Distinctions Best orator of the year 1953-54 Roll of Honour

Social and cultural activities:
Society, Club V.President. BAZM-I-URDU, Office
" PSYCHOLOGICAL SOCIETY
Tutor's name and designation Ch. MOHAMMAD ALI, M.A. (Phil)
Tutor's remarks An intelligent, wideawake & smart youngman. was always popular. Can handle men & situations. Cooperating & relaxed. Bears a good moral character.
Tutor's signature and date.

*In block capitals.
†In figures and words.

PRINCIPAL
Principal
Talimul-Islam-College
Rabwah.

P.T.O.